A Decolonial Feminism

'A vibrant and compelling framework for feminism in our times.'
—Judith Butler

'A powerful tool of social transformation.'
—Djamila Ribeiro, Brazilian human rights activist and
author of *Nos, Madelenas: uma palavra pelo feminism*

'Incisive ... an invitation to reconnect with the utopian power of feminism.'
—Aurelien Maignant, *Fabula*

'A powerful work.'

—*Les Inrocks*

'Develops a critical perspective on feminism to reconsider the conditions
of possibility and purpose ... resituates feminism in a truly political,
emancipatory and critical dimension.'

—Jean-Philippe Cazier, *Diacritik*

'Essential for highlighting the current divisions within feminist political
agendas, and for collective reflection on a profound, radical transformation
of society ... Necessary reading.'

—*Axelle n°219*

A Decolonial Feminism

Françoise Vergès

Translated by
Ashley J. Bohrer with the author

First published 2019 as *Un féminisme décolonial* by La Fabrique Éditions
English language edition first published 2021 by Pluto Press
345 Archway Road, London N6 5AA

www.plutobooks.com

This book has been selected to receive financial assistance from English PEN's 'PEN Translates!' programme, supported by Arts Council England. English PEN exists to promote literature and our understanding of it, to uphold writers' freedoms around the world, to campaign against the persecution and imprisonment of writers for stating their views, and to promote the friendly co-operation of writers and the free exchange of ideas. www.englishpen.org

Supported using public funding by
ARTS COUNCIL ENGLAND

British Library Cataloguing in Publication Data
A catalogue record for this book is available from the British Library

ISBN   978 0 7453 4110 1   Hardback
ISBN   978 0 7453 4112 5   Paperback
ISBN   978 1 7868 0641 3   PDF
ISBN   978 1 7868 0642 0   EPUB
ISBN   978 1 7868 0643 7   Kindle

This book is printed on paper suitable for recycling and made from fully managed and sustained forest sources. Logging, pulping and manufacturing processes are expected to conform to the environmental standards of the country of origin.

Typeset by Stanford DTP Services, Northampton, England

Simultaneously printed in the United Kingdom and United States of America

Preface

"Who cleans the world?" was where this book started, and it led to an examination of feminist struggles in the context of a violent and brutal counter-revolution. The question was triggered by a strike of the black and brown women who clean Gare du Nord train station in Paris. It was not the first strike of that kind, nor the first time that we saw the racialization and feminization of underpaid and undervalued cleaning and care work, or that the role of social reproduction in capitalism was discussed. Yet that strike generated a desire to look again at cleaning in the context of #MeToo, Black Lives Matter, the denunciation of police violence and femicides, massive feminist demonstrations and strikes especially in the Global South, but also in the context of feminist racism,[1] imperialism, militaristic violence as a solution to social problems, and racial capitalism. Since then, the pandemic of Covid-19 has shown that the "production [...] of group-differentiated vulnerability to premature death" is a constant of racial capitalism. The pandemic has revealed deep inequalities and injustices in the access to health services, that the right to breathe is not a universal one, and the unsurprising yet enraging fact that the death rate has been higher among black, indigenous, brown and poor communities, communities that carry the weight of lost jobs and increased poverty while billionaires are becoming richer. The vocabulary of "war" has justified sending unprotected workers in "essential" jobs to the "frontline." Finally, it has shown again that making the world safe and clean for a few rests on the exploitation and dispossession of many, that extractivism remains the logic of cultural and economic imperialism, and that the division between lives that matter and lives that do not matter, perpetually redrawn, remains strong. It is in these concrete struggles that I anchor decolonial feminism, in the desire to smash sexism, racism, capitalism and imperialism, and "to change everything," as Veronica Gago has urged us to do.[2]

I wanted also to examine the role of what I call in this text, *civilizational feminism*, which I see as a specific strategy of the current counter-revolution. This feminism borrows the vocabulary and objectives of the colonial civilizing mission, modernizing the policy that Frantz Fanon summarized thus: "Let's win over the women and the rest will follow,"[3] by putting first and foremost "women's rights" at the center of global politics, hence offering arguments to neoliberalism and imperialism difficult to refute (who is for forced marriages, girls being sold, women being denied rights?). By suggesting that the defense of women's rights should justify armed interventions, restricted visa policies, and close surveillance of non-white families and of queer sexualities and genders, instead promoting a neutralized and pacified 'equality', civilizational feminism was finally able to occupy a full seat at the table of power, a place that it had been denied under colonialism and for which it had to show a willingness to carry the torch of imperialism. In France, this feminism, which started to be theorized by feminists on the Left in the late 1980s, had succeeded in criminalizing the veil and Islam. That law is now a central piece in the construction of a feminism that has set up an insurmountable gap between cultures that are *by nature* opened to the equality between women and men, and cultures that are *by nature* hostile to such equality (namely, Islam). The cultural argument hides racist and imperialist interests which I explore in this book. But civilizational feminism has also been playing a role in defining the "good" feminist (white or non-white) and naming the feminists who must be attacked. Hence, it may come as no surprise that in the attacks on decolonial theory and political antiracism, via petitions, articles or tweets, women of color constitute the majority of persons identified (some with a photograph) as dangerous, with no protest from white feminists.

Since this book's original publication in French, we have also learned that the emergence of this global pandemic and its consequences could not be separated from hyper-consumption, mega-farms, industrial waste management, privatization of public health, and the ways in which race, age, class, and gender intertwine to increase precarity and vulnerability. These entanglements mean that decolonial feminism must remain as close as possible to a method that pulls all the threads that simultaneously, yet not in a linear-cause-and-effect way, create wasted lives and wasted lands. Decolonial feminism accepts the existence of other feminisms; it does not wish to become *the* theory, but to facilitate transborder and international alliances.

This is why the question of "Who cleans the world?" has remained a central point of analysis in my recent work. Extractivism means the production of waste, of dilapidated lands, rivers, seas and oceans, animals, plants and peoples. It is an economy that leaves behind ruins, ravaged forests, spoiled soil and subsoil, and exhausted bodies left to die. If "waste," Fred Magdoff and Chris Williams have argued, is "a sign of capitalism's success,"[4] then I wanted to understand cleaning and caring within that economy of extraction, ruination and exhaustion and the repressive norms of hetero-patriarchy. This text, in a way, followed my attempt to explore the links between twentieth-century campaigns of birth control, of forced abortion and forced contraception of women of color, and of the ways in which colonial slavery and European colonialism had racially managed the reproduction of their workforce, of the bodies from which they extracted all the life energy until their premature deaths.[5] The decolonial feminism I defend seeks to bring to light a kaleidoscopic narrative encompassing broad swathes of time and territory and to valorize the unstoppable struggles that challenge the legacies of colonial slavery and racism amid a new age of endless wars. There will be no repairing of what has been made into waste without thinking first by whom and how cleaning will be done. Damage to bodies and lands runs deep, its scars present in souls, in waters and lands. We must hold together past, present and future, but without foreclosing the possibility of a *better future*.

This text was written from a particular position: from *within* the current struggle for total liberation, from a long commitment to anti-patriarchal, anti-racist, anti-capitalist and anti-imperialist struggle, and a long engagement with feminist theory and practices in the Global South. By starting with a women's strike, I wanted to show how it remaps "social conflict *in practice*, " how it "politicizes the precarity of existence as a sequence that is inseparable from dispossession and extraction,"[6] and thus constitutes a radical critique of civilizational feminism. By ending with a call for solidarity with those who clean the world, enunciated by a young Dalit, I wished to suggest that the struggle against the racialization of cleaning and caring, while imagining a decolonial politics of cleaning, caring and repairing, shows the way to construct a post-racist, post-capitalist and post-imperialist, thus post-hetero-patriarchal, world.

Françoise Vergès

Acknowledgments

I want to thank all the brave and courageous women who are fighting for justice, peace and dignity worldwide. Their struggles are a constant source of energy, joy and feminist love. My thanks to all the vibrant, generous and combative, mostly young, women who came to the presentation of my book in 2019 and, with their questions, pushed me to clarify and expand my thinking. Finally, my thanks to translator Ashley Bohrer, to Adam Bell and Charlotte Coombes, to my editor at Pluto David Shulman and to my Paris editor and friend, Stella Magliani-Belkacem.

Translator's Introduction

There are so many more calls to overcome the theory-praxis divide than there are texts that truly move past it. Françoise Vergès' *A Decolonial Feminism* is a rare example that weaves theory and activism together with a remarkable ease, perhaps due in part to her own history as both a scholar and an activist. Simultaneously clear and deep, charting new conceptual territory *and* its direct implications for activism, the text opens up new terrains for thought and action in line with decolonial and feminist principles. In particular, Vergès uplifts the knowledge that activists are already bringing to the world stage, appreciating their contributions (in the forms of popular writing and in strategic decision making) and their implications for how we think, understand, and conceptualize. The pages of this text remind us that the struggle is about both theory and politics at once: in order to engage in the hard, daily process of reshaping the world, we also need to reshape our ideas. But likewise, activist work itself allows us to see new things. In this sense, Vergès' perspective does not merely repeat the idea that theory and practice need to somehow come together; rather, she shows how our theories of capitalism, colonization, and heteropatriarchy are changed by understanding real attempts at resistance, and how our activist work can and should be shaped by a decolonial feminist horizon in this "never ending struggle" of the "daily work" of revolution (p. 5).

Too often, however, our critiques of capitalism and our activist work to overcome it overlook the centrality of coloniality and heteropatriarchy. Vergès powerfully reframes these efforts, demonstrating that in order to overcome capitalism, we need a decolonial feminist approach to both theory and practice.

Colonization was the condition of the possibility of the rise of global capitalism. Coloniality, the structural and embedded global power relations that remained after the elimination of many (not all) forms of direct colonization, remains the condition of the possibility of capitalism's continuity. Colonization's theft of labor, land, and lives provided the basis for global capitalism; it would have been impossible without the appropriation of land and resources, without the enslavement of millions of racialized people, without the introduction of a social fabric of white, European domination. In its current form, capitalism continues to grow and expand through the hyperexploitation of racialized people, the appropriation of land and resources, the administration of debt both individual and national, the imposition of structural adjustment and political governance through capitalist intergovernments like the IMF and the World Bank, the impunity of large multi-national corporations in their sheer brutality toward life, human and non-human alike.

Both colonization and capitalism are rooted in heteropatri-archy. The imposition of capitalist modes of life through the colonial process entailed also the imposition of what María Lugones calls "the colonial/modern gender system"[1]—the matrix of ideas in which: gender and sex are collapsed and reduced to a question of reproductive biology; that biology is always figured in binary terms; one side of that binary (male) is superior to the other (female) side; sexuality is acceptable only between one member of each side of that binary. When European colonizers sought to subordinate the world, they intended to eliminate the diversity of systems of gender, sex, and sexuality they encountered around the world. Often, the very fact of having a non-binary, non-patriarchal, and non-heterocompulsive social organization of sex, gender, and sexuality was used as 'proof' that Indigenous communities 'needed' to be dominated by colonization, disciplined into the capitalist economy, and 'civilized' through forced conversion to Christianity. The current context of coloniality is no less wedded to colonial heteropatriarchy, even if in the present, the regime has made room for a limited number of successful women and queers to bolster and administrate it. The constitution of exploitation, land seizure, structural adjustment, and more have highly gender-differentiated effects, and often, as in the hysteria about so-called overpopulation and birth rates, have distinctly gendered narratives and policies of brutality. All of this is to say, as Vergès reminds us, that "capital *is* a colonizer" (p. 15; emphasis mine). The systems of capitalism, colonization, racism, and heteropatriarchy aren't separate systems that collide or collude to produce the present moment; they are mutually interlocking and reciprocally constructive. Capital *is* a colonizer, just as it *is* heteropatriarchal and racist.

Heteropatriarchy was, of course, also central to the rise and reproduction of capitalism inside Europe and white colonial society. White women and queers faced and still face their own forms of exploitation and oppression through capitalism, but far too often white modes of resistance replay rather than uproot capitalism and colonization. For this reason, these limited critiques and equality projects are often called 'white feminism' (and, we might add, white queer theory). As Vergès describes, white feminism is not so named because white people espouse it (though this is surely also true), but because it reaffirms a white vision of the world, a white horizon of analysis, and is often mobilized, either explicitly or implicitly, to shore up white global domination. White feminism and white queer theory/activism often aim at full integration into the privileges and institutions of the Global North without grappling with how they are based in the continual domination of people of color in and beyond the Global South, producing homo and femonationalisms[2] rather than liberation. In failing to excise this colonial dimension from their 'feminisms', white feminism partakes in and reproduces the assumed civilizational superiority of the North.

This is why Vergès uses the term 'civilizational feminism' throughout the book, to foreground that white feminism is not only a racial project unfolding within national borders, but is a global sustainer of contemporary colonial capitalism. So often critiques of white feminism suffer from a methodological nationalism, taking issues of gender, race, and class to be bounded by the nation-state. But, of course, as decolonial feminisms have been arguing for centuries, oppression and exploitation are global phenomena that require analysis and activism with a planetary horizon.

Decolonial feminism is the name for overcoming the project of civilizational feminism. It embraces a project of global transformation beyond the limits of capitalism, liberalism, and the state. As a politics, decolonial feminism demands the abolition of these institutions in order to bring about a world of true liberation. As a theory, Vergès' decolonial feminism requires a fundamental shift in how we understand logics of exploitation and oppression and the institutions that reproduce them. It is not enough to take pre-existing theories of capitalism, liberalism, and the state, and to simply 'add colonized women and stir.' Rather, we need to fundamentally rethink the meaning, histories, and logics of these terms.

Nowhere is this necessity more clearly articulated than in relationship to capitalism. Vergès re-grounds critiques of capitalism in the voices and experiences of the hyper-exploited, (post)colonized women who often receive capitalism's most pointed brutalities. Rather than proceed, as so many others do, from the assumption that a Marxist understanding of coloniality is about *expanding* an already-constituted analysis to a new domain or to new subjects, Vergès rather encourages us to totally re-center our analyses of capitalism and to build an analysis of what capitalism is and how it works from the position of 'those who clean the world' (p. 78). For Vergès, social reproduction cannot remain an afterthought in critiques of capitalism, but rather must take its place as the grounding center.

The question of cleaning allows Vergès to highlight capitalism's double face: capitalism as material and toxic waste producer and the production of human beings as disposable. This disposability of human life goes far beyond a segmented class of surplus population or reserve army of labor. Disposability rather emerges as a condition to which oppressed groups are subjected. Disposability can be linked to various sites of labor in the capitalist process—for example, in the analysis of the racialized women who clean the world—but disposability always means something *more*, something in *excess* over a location in the chain of production; disposability is a qualitative character of devalued life that capitalism produces through a racialized and gendered coloniality.

Thus we could read Vergès' book as one centered on life against disposability. She retells the history of the rise of civilizational feminism to help us more clearly understand how even putatively feminist movements have contributed to the devaluation of life. She explores the long history of decolonial feminist activism to chart previous challenges to this regime of disposability. Unfortunately, even leftist movements have sometimes replayed this capitalist script, at times treating activists or even whole communities as "disposable life." (p. 16) Decolonial feminism in Vergès' eyes allows us to critique a capitalism that treats "humans as waste" (p. 16) and to push beyond models of organizing that, even despite themselves, replay this trope, so that we can build a world of liberation and justice for ourselves and the planet.

Building this world, Vergès argues, requires abandoning projects of demanded political unity in favor of a global movement toward revolution based in a multiplicity of struggles. She writes, "It is not a question of connecting elements in a systematic and ultimately abstract way, but of making the efforts to see if and what links exist. A multi-dimensional approach makes it possible to avoid a hierarchy of struggles based on a scale of urgency whose framework often remains dictated by prejudice." (pp. 20–1) She explores a vision of multidimensional organizing that resonates deeply with what Angela Davis calls 'movement intersectionality'[3] and what in my own work I unpack as 'relational solidarity.'[4] The question is not how to manufacture relationships, but to uncover and act on the relationships between people, between groups, between social locations, and between struggles. A coalitional praxis that combines a recognition of difference with the potential for coordinated, collective action. Here, unity does not come at the price of difference and difference does not entail atomization or further alienation. In Vergès' work, we can see how recognizing and understanding difference is the pre-condition for working together across difference. Denial has never worked as revolutionary strategy. Rather than assume the divisiveness of difference, focusing on how it can be, in the words of Audre Lorde, "a springboard for creative change."[5]

This insistence on difference allows us to understand the name of this project. That the title of this text is 'A' decolonial feminism, not 'the' or even just 'decolonial feminism' speaks to the internal heterogeneity of decolonial feminisms and their approaches to revolutionary change. As she writes, "A feminist cannot claim to possess 'the' theory and 'the' method" (p. 19); I don't think this is merely an epistemological problem; it's not that we can't know, from our limited and partial perspectives which is *the* right theory or method; but rather that a central part of the project of decolonial feminism is its commitment to multiplicity. There is no single theory nor single method that can save us all. The domination we face is multiple and our responses, both scholarly and activist, must be as well. Vergès' contribution to this project is profound and paradigm-shifting.

Translating this work has been formative for re-thinking my own approach to these questions as both a scholar and an activist, and I am personally so excited, as both a scholar and an activist, for this text and all of its contributions to be available to Anglophone audiences for the first time.

The work of translation, like theory and activism, is never a singular, personal endeavor. This task would never have been completed without a network of collaborators and co-conspirators. I extend my profound gratitude to the following people for their help in this project: Julia Seguier, Gil Morejón, Michael Peterson, Claire Brault Sagan, Agatha Slupek, and Andrés Fabián Henao Castro.

Ashley J. Bohrer

floors, toilets, and restaurants have been cleaned and made available to them. This work, indispensable to the functioning of any society, must remain invisible. We must not be aware that the world we move around in is cleaned by racialized and overexploited women. On the one hand, this work has been considered what women must do (without complaint) for centuries; women's caring and cleaning work is free labor. On the other hand, capitalism inevitably creates invisible work and disposable lives. The cleaning industry is an industry that is dangerous to one's health: everywhere and for everyone who works in it. It is on these precarious lives, these endangered lives, these worn-out bodies, that the comfortable life of the middle class and the world of the powerful ultimately rests.

The workers' victory at the Gare du Nord was significant because it highlighted the existence of an industry in which race, feminization, exploitation, endangered health, invisibility, under-qualification, low wages, sexual- and gender-based violence and harassment are combined. Yet, in January 2018, on the front page of the media in France and elsewhere, appeared a petition signed by a group of 100 women, including Catherine Millet, Ingrid Caven, and Catherine Deneuve, denouncing "man-hating" within feminism.[5] The statement provoked debates and controversies, petitions and counter-petitions. The signatories denounced the #Balancetonporc[6] and #MeToo campaigns in which women call out men who have sexually harassed them. The petition accuses these movements of constituting a "campaign of denunciation," and of "summary judgment" since some men were "sanctioned in the course of their work, forced to quit, etc., when all they did was touch a knee, try to steal a kiss, talk about 'intimate' things at a business dinner or send a message with sexual connotation when the attraction was not reciprocated." They refer to a "wave of purification." That this letter garnered such attention is not surprising. The comfortable life of bourgeois women around the world is possible because millions of exploited and racialized women maintain this comfort by making their clothes, cleaning their homes and the offices where they work, taking care of their children, and by taking care of the sexual needs of their husbands, brothers, and partners. They thus have all the time in the world to sit around discussing the merits (or lack thereof) of being "bothered" in the metro or of aspiring to become a CEO. Certainly, men also benefit from the North/South division, and other men are put in the position of maintaining it. But looking at the role of women from the Global South in this world order, and in the international division of labour, highlights how their struggle challenges racial capitalism and heteropatriarchy.

I

Taking Sides:
Decolonial Feminism

The turn in feminism, from being long condemned by right-wing ideologies, to becoming one of their spearheads, is worthy of analysis. What is at stake in this ideological deployment? How did this change occur? How did we move from a feminism that was indifferent or ambivalent to racial and colonial issues in the Francophone world, to a white and imperialist feminism? What is femonationalism all about? How has feminism become, in a significant convergence, one of the pillars of several ideologies—liberal, nationalist-xenophobic, extreme right-wing—that, at first glance, are opposed to one another? How has the issue of women's rights become one of the trump cards played by the state and imperialism, one of neoliberalism's last recourses, and the spearhead of the civilizing mission of white, bourgeois feminism? This feminism and these xenophobic-nationalist currents do not profess to having shared objectives, but they do share common *points of convergence*, and it is these that interest us here.[1]

This book wishes to be a contribution to the critical works of feminists in the Global South and their allies in the North on gender, feminism, women's struggles, and the critique of civilizational feminism. I call this feminism 'civilizational' because, in the name of an ideology of women's rights, it has undertaken the mission of imposing a unique perspective that contributes to the perpetuation of domination based on class, gender, and race. I defend a decolonial feminism whose objective is the destruction of racism, capitalism, and imperialism, an agenda I will try to define more clearly.

"Feminism involves so much more than gender equality. And it involves so much more than gender," Angela Davis explains.[2] It also goes beyond the category of 'women' based on biological determinism, and it restores a radical political dimension to the notion of women's rights: taking into account the challenges faced by a humanity threatened with extinction. I take a stance against a temporality that describes liberation only in terms of unilateral 'victory' against the reactionary. Such a perspective shows an "enormous condescension of posterity"[3] towards those who are defeated. Writing history this way turns the story of oppressed peoples' struggles into one of successive defeats, imposing a linearity in which any setback is taken as proof that the fight was badly conducted (which is, of course, possible), rather than one that exposes the determination of reactionary and imperialist forces to crush any dissent. This is what songs of struggle—Black spirituals, revolutionary songs, gospel songs, songs of slaves and colonized people—recount: the long road to freedom, a never-ending struggle, revolution as daily work. It is in this temporality that I situate decolonial feminism.

Reclaiming Feminism

The term 'feminist' is not always easy to claim. The betrayals of Western feminism are its own deterrent, as are its heartless desire to integrate into the capitalist world and take its place in the world of predatory men and its obsession with the sexuality of racialized men and the victimization of racialized women. Why call yourself 'feminist,' why defend feminism, when these terms are so corrupted that even the far right can appropriate them? What do you do when the words 'feminist' and 'feminism' are now part of the arsenal of the modernizing neoliberal right wing when, even just a decade ago, they still held radical potential and were lobbed as insults? When, in France, a Minister organizes a "University of Feminism"[4] event in which the majority of the audience is female and claims to be feminist, yet they still jeer at a young, veiled woman and let a man lecture them for 25 minutes (roundly condemned only on Twitter)? What is feminism about once it becomes an exercise in appeasement? If feminism and feminists are in the service of capital, the state, and empire, is it still possible to breathe life back into them, by reanimating the movement with the objectives of social justice, dignity, respect, and the politics of life against the politics of death? But shouldn't we also defend feminism against the onslaught of fascist forces? When rape and murder are not only acceptable but also encouraged weapons to discipline women? When even being a blond woman, a mother, married to a man, a university professor, conforming to all of the standards of white, middle-class respectability, is no protection against the explosion of hatred, as we saw with the hearing of Christine Blasey Ford during the debates on the appointment of Brett Kavanaugh to the United States Supreme Court? Or when various governments across the world turn feminism into an anti-national ideology, foreign to 'the culture of the nation,' to better repress women? For a long time, I did not call myself a feminist; instead I described myself as an anti-colonial and anti-racist activist in women's liberation movements. I have been led to call myself a feminist, on the one hand because of the re-emergence of a feminism based in broad, transnational, pluralist, decolonial politics, and on the other because of the capture of women's struggles by civilizational feminism.

An Anti-Colonial Trajectory

Biography does not explain everything, and often, it does not explain very much at all, but in a book on feminism I owe it to myself to say something about my own trajectory, not because it is at all exemplary, but because women's struggles have played a major role in it. I was, for many years, an activist inside women's liberation groups; these struggles were always linked to more general liberation projects, in my own case, to the liberation from post-1962 French colonialism. My interest, curiosity, and commitment to emancipatory struggles is grounded in the political and cultural education I received on Réunion Island.[5] As a little girl who was raised in a context where school, media, and cultural activities were all subject to the post-1962 French colonial order, my experience was exceptionally transnational. For a long time, I did not call myself a feminist activist, but rather a 'women's liberation activist'. I had the privilege of growing up in a family of feminist and anti-colonial communists, being surrounded by activists of different backgrounds, religions, and genders, who gave me an insight into the meaning of struggle and solidarity, and I discovered the joy and happiness of collective struggle. As a teenager, I was the kind of idealist who could not stand the idea of setback and defeat; I wanted heroism and the crushing of the enemy. My parents' answer to my naïve and sentimental idealism brought me back to earth: "They are brutes, fascists, scoundrels. You can't expect anything from them. They don't respect any rights, especially our right to exist." There was nothing defeatist in these remarks; rather, they contained a lesson on another temporality of struggle: iconic, though complex, images of the capture of the Winter Palace, of Castro's troops entering Havana, of the National Liberation Army in Algiers. These were powerful images capable of mobilizing my imagination; but if I stopped at these images, I risked living in perpetual disillusionment. Tomorrow, the struggle would continue. I also learned very early on that if the state wants to crush a movement, it will use all the means and resources at its disposal both to repress and to divide the oppressed. With one hand it strikes and with the other, it tries to assimilate. Fear is one of the state's favorite weapons to produce conformity and consent, and I quickly understood the price to be paid for defying these rules, summarized thus: "Don't stand out, don't protest too much, and you won't get into trouble." The Debré Ordinance of 1960[6] demonstrated this in exiling 13 anti-colonial Réunionese activists (including union leaders). The message was clear: all dissident voices would be punished. The Réunionese historian Prosper Ève has spoken of "the island of fear" to analyze how slavery, post-slavery, and postcolonialism spread fear as a disciplinary technique well into the 1960s (and, I would add, to this day).[7] Fear is certainly not exclusive to the colonial system, but we should remember that colonial slavery was based on the constant threat of torture and death of human beings who were legally transformed into objects, and on the public spectacle of putting them to death. I learned also that one must use the laws of the state against the state itself, but without illusion or idealism, as understood by the enslaved women who fought to win free status, which they passed on to their children, or by the colonized people who used the colonial state's own laws against it (demanding freedom of the press, freedom of association, the right to vote, etc.). This strategy was always accompanied by a critique of the racial colonial state and its institutions. In other words, I understood that struggles are played on multiple fields and for objectives with different temporalities. The existence of a vast world where resistance and a refusal to yield to an unjust global order was part of the worldview that had been passed down to me. It was not when I arrived in France or went to university that

8

I discovered that capitalism, racism, sexism, and imperialism are fellow travelers, and I did not first encounter anti-colonial or anti-racist feminism by reading Simone de Beauvoir; I have been surrounded by it since early childhood.

The False Innocence of White Feminism

Following Frantz Fanon, who wrote, "Europe is literally the creation of the Third World," because it was built on plundering the world's wealth, and therefore "the wealth of imperialist countries is also our wealth,"[8] I can say that France is literally the creation of its colonial empire, and the North a creation of the South. I am therefore always surprised by the stubborn way in which slavery, colonialism, and everything related to the 'overseas' territories are overlooked in the analysis of contemporary France and the policies of its successive governments since the 1950s. Even more so than the colonial empire, the 'overseas' departments[9] (former slave societies or post-slave colonies) are excluded from contemporary history; no text on political issues, whether in philosophy, economy, or sociology, is interested in these remnants of the French colonial empire. This implies a desire to erase these peoples and their countries from the analysis of conflicts, contradictions, and resistance. What is the purpose of such repression if not to maintain the idea that all of this—slavery, colonialism, imperialism—certainly happened, but by being *outside* of France proper, it did not really matter? It undermines the links between capitalism and racism, between sexism and racism, and preserves French innocence. French feminism keeps its colonial and slave heritage at a distance. We are supposed to believe that since women are victims of masculine domination they have no responsibility for the racist policies deployed by the French State.

Feminism as a Struggle for the Right to Exist

To call oneself a decolonial feminist, to defend feminisms with decolonial politics today, is not only to tear the word 'feminism' out of the greedy hands of reactionaries' empty ideologies. It is also to affirm our fidelity to the struggles of the women of the Global South who have come before us. It is to recognize their sacrifices, honor their lives in all their complexity, the risks they took, and the difficulties and frustrations they experienced; it is to receive their legacy. On the other hand, it means recognizing that the offensive against women that is now openly justified and acknowledged by state leaders is not simply an expression of a brazen, masculinist dominance, but a manifestation of the destructive violence generated by capitalism. Decolonial feminism leads to de-patriarchalizing revolutionary struggles. In other words, feminisms with decolonial politics contribute to the struggle, undertaken for centuries by part of humanity, to assert its *right to existence*.

Feminisms with Decolonial Politics[10]

One of the significant developments of this still young twenty-first century, and one that has been growing in strength for several years, is the movement of decolonial feminisms the world over. This current has developed a multitude of practices, experiences, and theories; the most encouraging and original are the movements for land rights that address issues in a transversal and intersectional way. Unsurprisingly, this movement provokes violent reaction from heteropatriarchs, feminists in the North, and governments. It is in the Global South that these movements have developed, reactivating the memory of previous feminist struggles which have never been lost because they have never been abandoned, despite the terrible attacks against them. Joined by feminists in Spain,

France, and the United States, these movements declare war on racism, sexism, capitalism, and imperialism through mass demonstrations in Argentina, India, Mexico, and Palestine. These activists denounce rape and femicide, linking this struggle to the fight against policies of dispossession, colonization, extractivism, and the systematic destruction of the living.

This is not a 'new wave' or a 'new generation,' according to the favored formulas that mask the multiple lives of women's movements. It is rather a new stage in the process of decolonization, which we all know is a long historical process. These two formulas—wave and generation—contribute to erasing the long underground work that allows forgotten traditions to be reborn and obscures the fact that these currents have been buried; this metaphor also confers historical responsibility on a mechanism ('wave') or a demographic phenomenon ('generation'). Decolonial feminisms reject these segmenting formulas because these politics rest on the long history of the struggles of their elders: Indigenous women during colonization, enslaved women, Black women, women involved in the struggles for national liberation and the feminist subaltern internationalism of the 1950s–1970s, and racialized women who struggle daily even today.

Decolonial feminist movements, along with other decolonial movements and all movements for emancipation, are facing a period of acceleration in capitalism, which now regulates the functioning of its old accomplice, liberal democracy. These movements must find alternatives to economic absolutism and the infinite manufacture of goods. Our struggles are a threat to the authoritarian regimes that accompany the economic absolutism of capitalism. They also threaten masculinist domination, which is afraid of having to give up power—and which, everywhere, shows its proximity to fascistic forces. Our struggles also undermine civilizational feminism, which, having made women's rights into an ideology of assimilation and integration into the neoliberal order, reduces women's revolutionary aspirations to an equal share of the privileges granted to white men by white supremacy. As active accomplices of the racial capitalist order, civilizational feminists do not hesitate to support imperialist intervention policies, as well as Islamophobic and even "Negrophobic" policies.[11]

The stakes are high and the danger is dire. It is a question of opposing authoritarian nationalism and neo-fascism, both of which see racialized feminists as enemies to be destroyed. Western democracy will no longer even claim to protect us once the interests of capitalism are truly threatened. Capitalist absolutism encourages all regimes that allow it to impose its own rules and methods, open previously un-colonized spaces to it, and grant it access to the ownership of water, air, and land.

The rise of reactionaries of all kinds shows one thing loud and clear: a feminism that fights only for gender equality and refuses to see how integration leaves racialized women at the mercy of brutality, violence, rape, and murder, is ultimately complicit in it. This is the lesson to be learned from the election of a white man, supported by major landowners, the business world, and the evangelical churches, to the presidency of Brazil in October 2018. This is a man who openly declared his misogyny, homophobia, Negrophobia, and contempt for Indigenous people. This is a man who openly declared his willingness to sell Brazil to the highest bidder, to trample on social laws that protect the poorest classes and on those that protect nature, and to renege on the agreements signed with Amerindian peoples—and all of this came just a few months after the assassination of queer, Black, elected city councilor Marielle Franco. A simple approach to gender equality reveals its own limits when parties of the authoritarian right and

far-right elect women as leaders or choose them as muses—
Sarah Palin, Marine Le Pen, Giorgia Meloni...

Critique of Epistemicides

In Fernando Solanas' magnificent film *The Hour of the Furnaces* (1968), the following phrase appears: "the price we pay to be humanized." Indeed, the price we pay has always been high, and remains so. We are fighting against a system that has dismissed scientific knowledge, aesthetics, and entire categories of human beings as non-existent. Although the European world never succeeded in being completely hegemonic, it appropriated without hesitation or shame the knowledge, aesthetics, techniques, and philosophies of the people it enslaved and whose civilizations it denied. The rhetoric and practices of the colonial civilizing mission are still used to justify and legitimize the politics of theft. Without denying the complexities and contradictions of centuries of European colonialism (or what has escaped its surveillance techniques) and without overlooking the techniques of borrowing and *détournement* that colonized people have used as well, an in-depth understanding of South–South exchanges (cultural, technical, and scientific) is still lacking. In large part, this lack is due to research funding policies. The struggle for epistemic justice, which is to say, a struggle that demands equality between knowledges and contests the order of knowledge imposed by the West, is central. Decolonial feminisms are part of the long movement of scientific and philosophical reappropriation that is revising the European narrative of the world. They contest the Western-patriarchal economic ideology that turned women, Black people, Indigenous people, and people from Asia and Africa into inferior beings marked by the absence of reason, beauty, or a mind capable of technical and scientific discovery. This ideology has provided the basis for development policies that essentially say: "You are underdeveloped, but you can be developed if you adopt our technologies, our ways of solving social and economic problems. You must imitate our democracies, the best system, because you do not know what freedom, respect for the law, or the separation of powers is." This ideology nourishes civilizational feminism which says, in essence, to women: "You don't have freedom. You don't know your rights. We will help you reach the right level of development." The work of rediscovering and valuing knowledge, philosophies, literature, and imagination does not begin with us, but one of our missions is to make the effort to know and disseminate them. Feminist activists know the transmission of struggles can often be broken; they are often faced with ignorance of struggles and resistance movements. They often hear "our parents bowed their heads; they let themselves be pushed around." The history of feminist struggle is full of holes, approximations, and generalities. Decolonial feminist activists and academics have understood the need to develop their own modes of transmission and knowledge; through blogs, films, exhibitions, festivals, meetings, artworks, pieces of theater and dance, song, and music, through circulating stories and texts, through translating, publishing, and filming, they have made their movements and the historic figures of those movements known. It is a movement that should be highlighted, in particular, by making the effort to translate texts from the African continent, Europe, the Caribbean, South America, and Asia into many languages.

What Is Coloniality?

Among the main avenues of struggle pursued by a decolonial feminism, it is necessary first of all to highlight the fight against police violence and the accelerated militarization of society. These are underpinned by an idea of protection entrusted to the army and a classed/racialized concept of justice that the police are tasked with carrying out. This implies rejecting carceral and punitive feminism, which is satisfied with a judicial approach to violence that does not question the deaths of racialized women and men, since it is considered 'natural,' a cultural fact, an accident, or just a sad occurrence in our democracies. Efforts must be made to denounce systemic violence against women and transgender people, but we must do so without pitting victims against each other; we must analyze the production of racialized bodies without forgetting violence against transgender people and sex workers. We must de-nationalize and decolonize the narrative of white, bourgeois feminism without obscuring internationalist, anti-racist feminist networks. We must be attentive to policies of cultural appropriation and be wary of powerful institutions' attraction to 'diversity.' We should not underestimate the speed with which capital is able to absorb ideas and turn them into empty slogans. Why wouldn't capital be able to incorporate the idea of decolonization or decoloniality? Capital is a colonizer; the colony is consubstantial with it. In order to understand the colony's endurance, it is necessary to free oneself from an approach that sees the colony exclusively through the form Europe gave it in the nineteenth century. It is also necessary not to confuse colonization with colonialism. Peter Ekeh makes this helpful distinction: colonization is an event or a period, while colonialism is a process or a movement, a total social movement whose perpetuation is explained by the persistence of social formations resulting from this order.[12] Decolonial feminists study the way in which the complex of racism/sexism/ethnocentrism pervades all relations of domination, even when the regimes associated with these phenomena have disappeared. The notion of coloniality is extremely important for analyzing contemporary France, at a time when so, so many, even on the left, still believe colonialism is over. According to this narrative, decolonization simply put an end to colonialism. However, in addition to the fact that the Republic continues to have control over dependent territories, the institutions of power are still structured by racism. For decolonial feminisms in France, analyzing the coloniality of the French Republic remains central. It is a coloniality that inherits the division of the world that Europe traced in the sixteenth century and that has continually asserted through the sword, the pen, the faith, the whip, torture, threat, law, text, painting, and later, photography and cinema. It is a coloniality that establishes a politics of disposable life, of *humans as waste*.

However, we cannot limit our discussion to the space-time of the European narrative. The history of decolonization is also that of the longstanding struggles that have shaken up the world order. Since the sixteenth century, people have fought against Western colonization (for example, the struggles of Indigenous peoples and enslaved Africans, and the Haitian Revolution). Moreover, erasing the South–South transfers and routes of liberation and obscuring the internationalist experiences of anti-colonial forces suggests that decolonization has meant nothing more than independence under the law, and even that decolonization is a ploy. Ignorance of the circulation of people, ideas, and emancipatory practices within the Global South preserves the hegemony of the North–South axis; and yet, South–South exchanges have been crucial for the spread of dreams of liberation. These spatio-temporal re-readings are essential to stimulate the imagination of decolonial feminists.

Against Eurocentrism

To give our criticism the necessary scope, we must go so far as to say that civilizational feminism is born with the colony, insofar as European feminists develop a discourse of their own oppression by comparing themselves to slaves. The metaphor of slavery was a powerful one, for weren't women the property of their fathers and husbands? Were they not subordinated to the sexist laws of the church and the state? But, European Enlightenment feminism did not recognize the women who participated in the Haitian Revolution (which would be subsequently celebrated by the Romantic poets), nor did it recognize the enslaved women who revolted, resisted, or participated in *marronnage*.[13] The question here is not about passing judgment in retrospect, but about asking, in regard to this blindness and indifference, why the critical analysis of the racial genealogy of European feminism is still marginal. Rewriting the history of feminism from the colony is a central issue for decolonial feminism. We cannot simply consider the colony as a side issue of history. It is about considering that, without the colony, we would not have a France with structurally racist institutions. For racialized women in the North and the Global South, all aspects of their lives, the risks they face, the price they pay for misogyny, sexism, and patriarchy remain to be studied and made visible. To fight against femoimperialism is to bring the lives of 'anonymous' women back from silence, to reject the process of pacification, and to analyze why and how women's rights have become an ideological weapon in the service of neoliberalism (which can also fully support a misogynistic, homophobic, and racist regime). When women's rights are reduced to the defense of individual freedom—'to be free to, to have the right to...'—without questioning the content of this freedom, without questioning the genealogy of this notion in European modernity, we are entitled to wonder whether all these rights were granted because other women were not free. The narrative of civilizational feminism continues to be contained in the space of European modernity and never takes into account the fact that it is based on the denial of the role of slavery and colonialism in its own formation. The solution is not giving a place (even a marginal one) to enslaved, colonized, and racialized women, or those from overseas. What is on the agenda is how Western feminisms have been imbued with the division of the world that slavery and colonialism have enacted since the sixteenth century (between a humanity that has the right to live and one that can die). If feminism remains based on the division between women and men (a division that precedes slavery), but does not analyze how slavery, colonialism, and imperialism affect this division—nor how Europe imposes its conception of the division between women and men on the peoples it colonizes or how this division creates others—then this feminism is racist. Europe remains its center, and all its analyses begin from this part of the world: the colonial roots of fascism are forgotten, racial capitalism is not a category of analysis, enslaved and colonized women are not perceived as constituting the negative mirror-image of European women. Rare are the European feminists who have been resolutely anti-racist and anti-colonial. There have, of course, been exceptions—journalists, lawyers, activists who declared their solidarity with colonized people, but it has not constituted the basis of French feminism, despite its indebtedness to anti-racist struggles. Even the support for the Algerian nationalists that has been so important to French feminists has not led to an analysis of the boomerang effect described by Aimé Césaire in *Discourse on Colonialism*: "Colonization works to decivilize the colonizer."[14] Speaking of civilizational feminism or white, bourgeois feminism, has in this sense, a very specific meaning. It is not 'white' simply because white women adopt it, but because it claims to belong to the part of the world, Europe, that was built on a racialized division of the world. It is bourgeois because it does not attack racial capitalism. We are entitled to ask this question: how, why, and by what means could European feminism have avoided being affected by centuries of racial laws, imperialist domination, and the ideology of white supremacy? Since racism is too often conflated with the extreme right, pogroms, and ghettos in Europe, we often do not pay enough attention to the extent to which racism also spread and disseminated quietly and dispassionately, through the naturalization of the state of racialized servitude and the idea that some civilizations have been incompatible with progress and the rights of women. Saving racialized women from 'obscurantism' remains one of the main principles of civilizational feminisms. This policy was aimed at women in the colonies and at racialized and working-class women domestically. We cannot deny that for some, these actions were based on a desire to do the 'right thing,' they were driven by a strong belief in the righteousness of their feelings and of their desire to improve the condition of women; nor can we deny that some colonized people benefited from their actions. But there is a difference between aid and radical criticism of colonialism and capitalism, and between aid and fighting against exploitation and injustice. Or, to quote Australian Indigenous activist Lilla Watson: "If you have come to help me, you are wasting your time. But if you have come because your liberation is bound up with mine, then let us work together."[15]

For a Critical Decolonial Pedagogy

The theories and practices forged within the anti-racist, anti-capitalist, and anti-colonial struggles are invaluable resources. Decolonial feminisms bring the following to other struggles that share the goal of re-humanizing the world: their library of knowledge, their experience of practices, and their anti-racist and anti-sexist theories, which are thoroughly linked to anti-capitalist and anti-imperialist struggles. A feminist cannot claim to possess *the* theory and *the* method;

she seeks to be multidimensional and intersecting. She asks herself what she does not see, she seeks to deconstruct the malignance of school education that has taught her not to see, feel, or know how to read, but to suffocate her senses, be divided within herself and be separated from her world. She must relearn how to hear, see, and feel in order to be able to think. She knows that the struggle is collective, and she knows that the determination of her enemies to defeat liberation struggles must not be underestimated, that they will use all the weapons at their disposal—censorship, defamation, threats, imprisonment, torture, and murder. She also knows that the struggle brings difficulties, tensions, and frustrations, but also joy and gaiety, discovery and expansion of the world.

Decolonial feminism is a feminism that offers a multidimensional analysis of oppression and refuses to divide race, sexuality, and class into mutually exclusive categories. Multidimensionality, a concept proposed by Darren Lenard Hutchinson, responds to the limits of the notion of intersectionality in order to better understand how "racist and heteronormative power not only creates precise exclusions at the intersection of domination, but shapes all social proposals and subjectivities,"[16] including among those who are privileged. This notion echoes the 'feminism of totality,' a methodology that aims to take into account the *totality* of social relationships.[17] I share the importance given to the state and I adhere to a feminism that thinks about patriarchy, the state, *and* capital; reproductive justice, environmental justice, *and* criticism of the pharmaceutical industry; the rights of migrants, refugees, *and* the end of femicide; the fight against the Anthropocene, racial Capitalocene, *and* the criminalization of solidarity. It is not a question of connecting elements in a systematic and ultimately abstract way, but of making the effort to see if, and what, links exist. A multidimensional approach makes it possible to avoid a hierarchy of struggles based on a scale of urgency whose framework often remains dictated by prejudice. The challenge is to hold several threads at once, to override ideologically induced segmentation, and "to grasp how production and social reproduction are historically articulated."[18] This approach has guided me in my analysis of the thousands of abortions and sterilizations perpetrated annually on Réunion Island in the 1970s. If I had stopped at an explanation that only blamed the white, French doctors who performed them, I would have reduced the story to one about greed among a few white men. Rather, a study of all the elements highlighted a French State policy of natalism in France and of anti-natalism towards the racialized and poor women in its 'overseas' departments, a policy that was part of a global reconfiguration of Western birth-control policies in the context of national liberation struggles and the Cold War.[19] Similarly, in a presentation of a critical decolonial pedagogy,[20] I used a familiar fruit, the banana, to shed light on a number of analogies and elective affinities: the banana's dispersion from New Guinea to the rest of the world, the banana and slavery, the banana and US imperialism (banana republics), the banana and agribusiness (pesticides, insecticides—the chlordecone scandal in the Antilles), the banana and working conditions (the plantation regimes, sexual violence, repression), the banana and the environment (monocultures, polluted water and land), the banana and sexuality, the banana and music, the banana and performance (Josephine Baker), the banana and branding (Banana Republic), the banana and racism (when did the association of bananas and Negrophobia begin?), the banana and science (researching the 'perfect' banana), the banana and consumption (bringing bananas into the home, suggesting recipes), the banana and rituals for ancestors, and the banana and contemporary art. The method is simple: starting from one element to uncover a political, economic, cultural, and social ecosystem in order to avoid the segmentation that the Western social-science method has imposed. The most enlightening and productive analyses in recent decades have been those that have drawn the greatest number of threads together to highlight the concrete and subjective networks of oppression that weave the web of exploitation and discrimination.

Decolonial Feminism as a Utopian Imaginary

In the context of a capitalism with increased destructive power, of racism, and of murderous sexism, this book affirms that, yes, feminism, which I call *decolonial feminism*, must be defended, developed, affirmed, and put into practice. *Maroon feminism* offers decolonial feminism a historical anchor in the struggles to resist the slave trade and enslavement. All the initiatives, actions, gestures, songs, rituals that night or day, hidden or visible, represent a radical promise, I understand as 'maroon'. *Marronnage* affirmed the possibility of a future, even when one was foreclosed by law, church, state, and culture, all of which proclaimed that there was no alternative to slavery, that slavery was as natural as day and night, that the exclusion of Blacks from humanity was a *natural* thing. The maroons tore the veil of lies by revealing the fictional aspect of these naturalizations. They created sovereign territories at the very heart of the system of slavery and proclaimed their freedom. Their dreams, their hopes, their utopias, as well as the reasons for their defeats, remain spaces we can turn to in order to think about action. Therefore, it is a utopia, in the sense of a radical promise, that constitutes a space from which to attack capitalism's proclamation that there is no alternative to its economy and ideology, that it is as natural as day and night, and its promises that technological and scientific solutions will transform its ruins into spaces of happiness. Against these ideologies, *marronnage* as a politics of disobedience affirms the existence of a futurity, to borrow a concept from Black American feminists. In claiming *marronnage*, feminism anchors itself in questioning the naturalization of oppression; by claiming to be decolonial, it fights the coloniality of power. But is using the term 'feminism' the appropriate response to the rise of political fascism, capitalist predation, and the destruction of the ecological conditions necessary for living beings? Or to the policies of dispossession, colonization, erasure and commodification, and criminalization and imprisonment as responses to an increase in poverty? Does it even make sense to dispute the terrain civilizational feminism occupies—also called *mainstream* or white, bourgeois feminism—which envisions correcting injustices by sharing equal positions between women and men (without questioning the organization of society, economics, or culture), and tries to make gender, sex, class, origin, and religion into an entirely private matter—or into a commodity? Fighting femonationalism and femoimperialism (I develop their content below) seems reason enough for defending a decolonial feminism. But that is not enough. The essentialist argument of a female nature that would be better able to respect life and would desire a just and egalitarian society does not hold: women are a political category neither spontaneously nor in themselves. What justifies a reappropriation of the term 'feminism' is that its theories and practices are rooted in the awareness of a profound, concrete, daily experience of oppression produced by the state–patriarchy–capital matrix, which manufactures the category of 'women' to legitimize policies of reproduction and assignment, both of which are racialized.

Decolonial feminisms do not aim to improve the existing system but to combat all forms of oppression: justice for women means justice for all. It does not hope naïvely, nor does it feed on resentment or bitterness; we know that the road is long and fraught with pitfalls, but we keep in mind the courage and resilience of racialized women throughout history. This is not a new wave of feminism, but the continuation of the struggles for the emancipation of women in the Global South.

Decolonial feminisms draw on the theories and practices that women have forged over time in anti-racist, anti-capitalist, and anti-colonial struggles, helping to expand theories of liberation and emancipation around the world. It is about firmly combatting police violence and the accelerated militarization of society, along with the conception of security that entrusts the army, class/race-based machine of justice, and the police with the task of ensuring it. It rejects carceral and punitive feminism.

In this cartography of struggle of women in the South, colonial slavery still plays a foundational role in my view. It constitutes the "matrix of race" to use philosopher Elsa Dorlin's apt phrase.[21] Slavery links the history of wealth accumulation, plantation economics, and rape (the basis of a reproductive policy in the colony) to the history of the systematic destruction of social and family ties, and to the race/class/gender/sexuality knot. The European temporality of slavery/abolition relegates colonial slavery to a historical past and therefore ignores how its strategies of racialization and sexualization continue to cast their shadows on our time. The immense contribution of Afro-feminism (Brazil, United States) to the importance of colonial slavery in the formation of the modern world, in the invention of the white world, and its role in the prohibition of family ties, has still not affected the analyses of white, bourgeois feminism. Feminists in the West have analyzed how 'good motherhood,' 'good mothers,' and 'good fathers' of the heteronormative family have been constructed, but always without taking account of the 'boomerang effects' of slavery and colonization. We know that under slavery, children could be taken from their mothers at any time, that mothers were not allowed to defend their children, that Black women were available to the children of their owners as wetnurses and nannies, that Black children were available to the master's children as companions or playmates, that Black girls and women were sexually exploited, and that all of these roles were subject to the whims of the master, his wife, and his children. Enslaved men were deprived of the social role of father and partner. This legally established destruction of family ties continues to hang over family policies targeting racialized minorities and Indigenous peoples.

White Women and Women of the Global South

White women do not like to be told they are white. To be white is to be constructed as a being so ordinary, so devoid of characteristics, so normal, so meaningless that, as Gloria Wekker points out in *White Innocence*,[22] it is practically impossible to make a white woman recognize that she is white. You tell her, and she's upset, aggressive, horrified, practically in tears. She finds your remark 'racist.' For Fatima El-Tayeb, arguing that modern European thought has given birth to race is an intolerable violation of what is dear to Europeans, the idea of a 'colorblind' continent, devoid of the devastating ideology that it has exported throughout the world.[23] The feeling of being innocent is at the heart of this inability to see themselves as white and thus protects them from any responsibility in the current world order. Therefore, there can be no *white* feminism (since there are no white women), only a universal feminism. The ideology of women's rights that civilizational feminism promotes could not be racist, since it comes from a continent free of racism. Before continuing, it should be reiterated— since any reference to the existence of whiteness leads to an accusation of 'reverse racism'—that it is not a question of skin color nor of racializing everything, but of admitting that the long history of racialization in Europe (through anti-Semitism, the invention of the 'Black race' and of the 'Asian race,' or the 'East') has not been without consequences for the conception of human beings, sexuality, natural rights, beauty, and ugliness. Admitting to being white—that is, admitting that privileges have historically been granted to this color—would be a big step. By privileges, I even mean ones as banal as being able to enter a store without being automatically suspected of wanting to steal, or not being systematically told that the apartment you want is already rented, or being naturally taken for the lawyer rather than the assistant, the doctor rather than the nurse, the actress rather than the cleaning lady. There are admittedly white women who have shown, and are showing, deep solidarity with anti-racist political struggles. But white women also need to understand how tiring it is, always having to educate them about their own history. After all, whole libraries on this topic are available to them. What is holding them back? Why are they waiting to be educated? Some say that we are forgetting about class, that racism was invented to divide the working class, that, paradoxically, we bolster the far-right by talking about 'race.' It is always up to racialized people to explain, justify, and accumulate the facts and figures, while neither facts, figures, nor moral sense change anything in the balance of power. Reni Eddo-Lodge expresses a familiar and legitimate feeling when she explains "why I am no longer talking to white people about race." Claiming that the debate on racism can take place as if the two sides were equal is illusory, she writes, and it is not for those who have never been the victims of racism to impose the framework of the discussion.[24]

The white woman was literally the product of the colony. Philosopher Elsa Dorlin explains how, in the Americas, the first naturalists took sexual difference as their model for the concept of 'race': Amerindians in the Caribbean or imprisoned slaves were taken to be populations with pathogenic, effeminate, or weak temperaments. The definition of a "sexual temperament" moved, Dorlin writes, to that of a "racial temperament." She concludes that the body-politics of the nation was grounded in the opposition between the feminine model of the "mother"—white, healthy, and maternal—and figures of a "degenerate" femininity—the witch, the enslaved African.[25] European women did not escape the epistemological division that took place in the sixteenth century and rendered a significant wealth of knowledge 'non-existent.'[26] In their view, women in the South were deprived of knowledge, a real concept of freedom, of what made up a family or constituted 'a woman' (not necessarily linked to gender or sex defined at birth). Perceiving themselves to be victims of men (and, indeed, they legally remained minors for centuries), European women do not see that their desire for equality with European men was based on the exclusion of racialized people. Nor do they see that the European conception of the world and modernity (of which they are themselves a part) relegated those who belonged neither to their class nor to their race to de facto and de jure inequality. When European women make their experience (often the experience of bourgeois women) universal, they contribute to dividing the world in two: civilized/barbarian, women/men, white/Black, and the binary conception of gender becomes universal. María Lugones has spoken of the "coloniality of gender": the historical experience of colonized women is not only that of racial devaluation,[27] she writes, but also of sexual assignment. Colonized women were reinvented as "women" in light of the norms, criteria, and discriminatory practices used in Medieval Europe.[28] Racialized women have therefore faced a double subjugation: that of colonizers and that of colonized men. The Nigerian feminist philosopher Oyèrónké Oyěwùmí also questions the universality of Euro-modern gender formations. She sees this universality as the manifestation of the hegemony of Western biologism and the domination of Euro-American ideology in feminist theory.[29]

Feminism and Its Repression of Slavery

By drawing an analogy between their situation and that of slaves, European feminists denounced a position of dependence, a status of minors-for-life. But in doing so they erased the central elements of slavery—capture, deportation, sale, trafficking, torture, denial of social and family ties, rape, exhaustion, racism, sexism, and death that framed the lives of female slaves—appropriating through analogy a condition that was not theirs. It is not denying the brutality of masculine domination in Europe to insist on its distinction from colonial slavery. The Enlightenment, the century of the publication of historical feminist texts for the European continent, is also the century when the Transatlantic Slave Trade peaked (70,000 to 90,000 Africans trafficked per year, whereas up until the eighteenth century, the figure was 30,000 to 40,000 per year). The (few) French abolitionist feminists of the eighteenth century used a sentimentalist vision, a literature of pity, to denounce slavery as a crime.[30] One of the most famous works of this genre, Olympe de Gouges' play *Zamore and Mirza*, gives a white woman the main role: it is she who performs the emancipation of Blacks from slavery. Renamed as *Negro Slavery or the Happy Shipwreck*[31] at the request of the Comédie Française in 1785, the play tells the story of a couple of two young maroons on the run taking refuge on a desert island. Zamore, who is a wanted man because he killed a commander who was harassing Mirza, rescues a young French couple from drowning, one of whom, Sophie, is the daughter of the island's governor, Saint-Frémont. Sophie helps Zamore and Mirza escape their enslavement by asking her father for mercy and at the end of the play, the governor frees them. Or, in summary, without the white woman, there would be no freedom. Even this play, timid in tone and content, nevertheless caused a scandal. It was considered subversive because the author suggested "a widespread freedom [that] would make the Negro race as essential as the white race" and that one day "they will cultivate freely their own land like the farmers in Europe and will not leave their fields to go to foreign nations."[32] This account, in which the intervention of whites changes the fate of enslaved Blacks, and in which Blacks must present qualities of gentleness, sacrifice, and submission to deserve freedom, was hegemonic. Only direct testimonies of former captives and slaves contested this narrative of white saviorism. In *Paul and Virginia*, one of the most widely read books of the eighteenth century, Bernardin de Saint-Pierre softened the nature of white–Black relations. One of the most stunning episodes of the novel features a young, enslaved woman who, having fled because she was mistreated by a slave-master, appears one Sunday morning in front of Virginia's house. The latter takes her in and feeds her before persuading her to return to her master's house and to apologize for running away. The young slave is brought back by sweet Virginia to her master, who, of course, punishes her.

Virginia's absurd naivete is the result of her 'innocent' refusal to acknowledge racism. She transforms slavery into a simple individual relationship where the master's gesture of forgiveness overcomes the violence of the enslaved. The testimonies left by female slaves absolutely contradict this absurdity with their accounts of the brutal consequences that white women refuse to see. In the nineteenth century, most feminists—with a few rare exceptions like Louise Michel and Flora Tristan—supported the colonial empire, which they saw as a lever for releasing colonized women from the shackles of sexism in their societies. They did not reject the civilizing mission; they only wanted to ensure that its feminine side would be respected. They created schools for colonized girls, encouraged service and domestic work, protested against abuse, but never attacked colonization itself. They accepted its structure and institutions, finding in the colony the possibility of deploying the principles and values of their feminism, which adhered to the colonial republican order. Faced with the colonists' hostility, they sublimated their actions. The study of travelers' journals and feminists' reports could make us forget that the military colonial conquest offered the terrain for their travels and their actions, that it is thanks to colonial armies that travel routes opened up, and that places for European women to live were built.

In the hegemonic account of women's rights struggles, one omission in particular highlights the refusal to consider the privileges of whiteness. The hegemonic story features women deprived of their rights who obtain them progressively, leading up to the right to vote, which is the hallmark of European democracies. But, although for a long period of time white women were effectively unable to enjoy many civil rights, they did have the right to own human beings; they owned slaves and plantations and, following the abolition of slavery, headed colonial plantations where forced labor was rampant.[33] They were not denied access to human property and were granted this right because they were white. One of the greatest enslavers on Réunion Island was a woman, Madame Desbassyns, who had neither the right to vote nor to sit for the baccalaureate,[34] nor to be a lawyer, doctor, or university professor, but she did have the right to own human beings, who were classified as chattel in her estate. As long as the history of women's rights is written without taking this privilege into account, it will be misleading.

Ignoring the role of enslaved women, female maroons, and colonized women workers who were committed to the struggles for freedom and racial equality, white, French feminism does establish the only framework for women's struggles. It aims at equality with bourgeois, white men and is confined to mainland France. Deafness and blindness towards the wellsprings of 'women's rights,' towards the role of colonialism and imperialism in their vision, could only feed an openly nationalist, unequal, and Islamophobic feminist ideology where the term 'French' comes to delineate, not a linguistic field as a common tool, but a national/imperial space.

What were the genders under slavery? Enslaved women were Black and women, but on the plantations all enslaved human beings were beasts of burden. In the eyes of slave owners, Black women were sexual objects and not human beings whose gender would require them to be treated with gentleness and respect. As slaves, their legal status was as objects and therefore they did not fully belong to humanity. In other words, gender does not exist in itself; it is a historical and cultural category, which evolves over time and cannot be conceived in the same way in the metropole and the colony, nor from one colony to another, or even within one colony. For racialized women, affirming what it means *to be a woman* has been a battleground. Women, as I said, are not a political class in itself.

French Exceptionalism: The Republic of Innocence

In France, where republican doctrine is confronted with the unthinkables of the colonial past and the challenges of the post-colonial present, bourgeois feminism (of Left and Right) has come to the rescue by identifying feminism with the Republic. It does not matter that women only obtained the most basic rights very late in the Republic; the latter is said to be naturally open to differences. The fact that these rights were obtained through costly struggles is erased; in this narrative, they come from above, from the natural generosity of the Republic. It is also forgotten that, while French women obtained the right to vote in 1944, this right was severely restricted in the so-called 'overseas' departments until the 1980s. Not all women living in the French Republic have automatically enjoyed the rights granted to white French women. But it is not only bourgeois women who are racists. In 1976, in the bulletin of a revolutionary group of factory women, women workers in Renault-Flins expressed their anti-Arab racism, adding that it was explained by "the reactionary attitude of Arabs [sic] towards women [and because of] prejudices ingrained in them by the bourgeoisie and which shock their principles: they are the first to be accommodated by the town councils. They do not want to leave their slums, they are dirty, if they returned to their country, there would be less unemployment in France."[35]

Even today, access to prenatal and postnatal care is not equally distributed; racialized women are more easily deprived of access to care, and they are more often victims of medical neglect, if not abuse. The May 2017 death of Naomi Musenga—a 27-year-old woman whose calls to emergency services not only went unanswered but were mocked—highlighted this racist discrimination. No institution appears to be free of structural racism: not schools, not the courts, not prisons, not hospitals, not the army, nor art, culture, or the police. If the debate on structural racism in France is so difficult, it is also because of a passion for abstract principles rather than for studying realities. Despite reports of racist/sexist discrimination even from government agencies, this blindness persists.

Another obstacle to the deracialization of French society is the narcissism maintained through notions of French singularity and exceptionalism. The French language is still presented in the twenty-first century as a vector of the civilizing (feminist) mission because it supposedly carries within it the idea of equality between women and men. It is this reasoning that justifies the priority given to young African women in obtaining government scholarships.[36] However, language is not neutral, and racism has crept into it. The history of words that begin with 'N' in both feminine and masculine, and which are racist insults, is insightful in this regard. By the end of the eighteenth century, the 'N-word' had fully taken on the meaning of 'Black slave' and the N-word and *Black* were used interchangeably. A legitimate question then arises: by what miracle could feminism's vocabulary have remained untouched by racism? Let us take the example of Hubertine Auclert, one of the great figures of nineteenth-century French republican feminism, known for her tireless struggle for women's suffrage, against the Napoleonic code which had made women legal minors and subjects to their husbands, and against the death penalty. Secretary of the newspaper *L'avenir des femmes* (*Women's Future*), she adopted Victor Hugo's formula, 'women: those I call slaves,'[37] studied the role of women in revolutions, and denounced "the slavery of women."[38] Laurence Klejman and Florence Rochefort, authors of a 1989 book on French feminism, summarize her struggle as follows:

> She drew all her political training from feminism and, impatient, she revolted against her elders who were content either with a principled demand or who simply refused to take women's suffrage seriously because of the danger that this reform would represent for the regime. She chose provocation as her tactic. Astute and imaginative, she immediately asserted a political identity through various acts of civil disobedience: voter registration, tax strikes, refusing the census on the grounds that if French women do not vote, they should not pay tax or be counted either.[39]

In 1881, she founded her own newspaper, *La Citoyenne* (*The Female Citizen*), in which she demonstrated that the principles of the Republic were being flouted, argued that Bastille Day was a celebration of masculinity, and considered the Napoleonic code as a remnant of the monarchy. For Auclert, a dividing line existed: *the color line*. In her text "Women are the Negroes [sic]," she protested against the fact that the right to vote was granted to Black men in the colonies after the abolition of slavery in 1848: "The step given to savage negroes, over the cultured white women of the metropole, is an insult to the white race." The right to vote was colored by the feminist pen: "If negroes vote, why don't white women?" "In our distant possessions," she continued, "Black men, who are not interested in our ideas or our affairs, vote. However, we deny the vote to enlightened women in the metropole, when it would prevent them from being crushed by the burden of social constraints." The *coloring* of suffrage reveals the force of racist prejudice for this feminist: "This comparison between half-savage 'negroes,' who have neither responsibilities nor obligations, voting, and civilized women, taxpayers and non-voters, more than abundantly demonstrates that men retain their omnipotence over women only in order to exploit their disadvantage." It is therefore necessary "to prevent Frenchmen from treating French women as 'negroes'."[40] Opposing enlightenment to obscurantism replays the old opposition between civilization and barbarism, but it is above all, accepting the racialization of feminism. The universal is very difficult to hold on to.

Women in French Colonialism

Frantz Fanon describes the role that twentieth-century colonialism gave to colonized women thus: "At an initial stage, there was a pure and simple adoption of the well-known formula, 'Let's win over the women and the rest will follow.'" He continues,

This enabled the colonial administration to define a precise political doctrine: 'if we want to destroy the structure of Algerian society, its capacity for resistance, we must first of all conquer the women; we must go and find them behind the veil where they hide themselves and in the houses where the men keep them out of sight. It is the situation of woman that was accordingly taken as the theme of action. The dominant administration solemnly undertook to defend this woman, pictured as humiliated, sequestered, cloistered. It described the immense possibilities of woman, unfortunately trans-formed by the Algerian man into an inert, demonetized, indeed dehumanized object. The behavior of the Algerian was very firmly denounced and described as medieval and barbaric. With infinite science, a blanket indictment against the 'sadistic and vampirish' Algerian attitude toward women was prepared and drawn up. Around the family life of the Algerian, the occupier piled up a whole mass of judgments, appraisals, reasons, accumulated anecdotes, and edifying examples, thus attempting to confine the Algerian within a circle of guilt.[41]

This ideology feeds twenty-first-century civilizational feminism: negrophobic and orientalist representations, pre-conceived ideas about *the* oriental or African family, and about the mother and father in these families. Social reality has no place in this ideology because it would then become necessary to analyze the human and economic catastrophe that French republican colonial policies have caused in the colonies.[42] The terrain on which civilizational feminism has developed and garnered the attention of the powerful is multiple: the French Army's attempts to unveil Algerian women; the representation of Algerian women combatants as victims (either of the Army or their fellow male fighters, but never as beings making a free choice); the indifference to the way that republican coloniality oppresses women of the overseas territories and racialized women in France; the refusal to denounce capitalism; the faith in European modernity.

The fear inspired by women's participation in national liberation movements has led to a mobilization of international institutions, foundations, and ideologues which shape discourses and develop practices, including those based on repression. This is precisely how the notions of development and 'women's empowerment' were spread, just as the discourse of 'women's rights' had been. The latter, which emerged as a feminist technique of discipline in the late 1980s—at the same time as the discourses of the 'end of history' and the 'end of ideologies'—would be propelled by multiple developments throughout the late twentieth and early twenty-first centuries.

Developmentalist Feminism

Since the 1970s, international institutions and North American foundations have been active in channeling and steering feminist movements. The 1970s was a decade that saw the entrance of millions of women into the realm of paid work. The transformations of capitalism were decisive moments in bringing about an explosion of low wages and precarity, notably through the worldwide so-called feminization of under-skilled jobs in open economic zones and in the informal economy. During this decade, the progressive feminization of employment went hand in hand with a very clear increase in global inequalities. The conflict between a revolutionary approach to women's liberation and an anti-discrimination approach, which seeks reform within the law and women's integration into capitalism, has thus intensified. The revolutionary approach does not reject the struggle for reforms but it does reject the argument that renders women's entry into the realm of paid work as an opportunity to gain individual autonomy; the revolutionary approach proposes collective organization in the workplace instead. In the anti-discrimination approach, independence is measured by the capacity to access consumption and individual autonomy (recall the image of the 'corporate woman' and the accompanying trend of blazers with shoulder pads). Lastly, the 1970s was also the decade of the global deployment of anti-natal policies that targeted Third World women. The United States led this effort through financial support of birth control in racialized communities domestically and in South America. In a document that had long been confidential, the National Security Administration clearly exposed the reasons for this policy—too many youths would want to emigrate, thus threatening the security of the free world—and recommended that the federal agency be entrusted with it.[43] In France, sterilization and abortions in the 'overseas' departments were encouraged by the government.[44]

It was not, however, the United States, its government, or its mainstream feminist movement that sought to raise the issue of women's rights at the international level, but rather the Soviet Union and Third World countries. In the early 1970s, they proposed that the United Nations organize a "Decade for Women." Programmed to start in 1975, its aim would be to "ensure women's ownership and control of property, as well as improvements in women's rights with respect to inheritance, child custody and loss of nationality," to affirm that "women's rights are an integral part of human rights," and to "promote gender equality and end violence against women."[45] But these rather modest objectives would be soon discarded in favor of promoting women's entry into the neoliberal order. Indeed, though the US government was initially suspicious of the initiative—as ever, birth control remained the primary basis of their interest in the Third World—by 1979, President Carter announced that for the American government "the key objective of U.S. foreign policy is to advance worldwide the status and conditions of women."[46] In France, the creation of a State Secretariat for Women's Rights in 1974 indicated the institutionalization of feminism. Women's rights were gradually stripped of their political significance. Yet, things did not go exactly as planned at the four major meetings of the Decade for Women—Mexico City (1975), Copenhagen (1980), Nairobi (1985), and Beijing (1995).[47] The movement to collect information about women around the world largely supported by governments announced the focus on accumulating data and reports and on consolidating the existence of expertise on women's rights. In Copenhagen, feminists from North African and Sub-Saharan countries challenged the terms 'savage customs' and 'backwards cultures' used by Western feminists denouncing female mutilations, genital infibulation, or what they saw as other violations of human rights, and analyzed this insistence as a desire to westernize women's struggles. In Nairobi, the opposition to the occupation of Palestine revealed the opposition between a decolonial feminism and a feminism that did not want to confront coloniality. Ultimately, the question of discrimination rather than of liberation took center stage. In Beijing, the return to order was made clear. Unlike the location of the official meeting in the city center, made fit for an assembly of dignitaries, the alternative forum where thousands of feminist NGOs and activists gathered was outside the city and lacking sufficient facilities.

Government negotiations were held behind closed doors.[48] While the situation of women around the world was worsening because of imperialism and capitalism, the civilizing feminist machine was being built. In her closing speech at the Beijing meeting, Hillary Clinton declared that women's rights were human rights, envisioned through a completely Western frame. Anti-colonial movements for national independence, which had emphasized the end of the exploitation of the Global South's resources, denounced a Western-dominated organization of information, and defended their own concept of health, education, and women's rights, were marginalized in favor of a discourse that refuses to question the structures of capitalism and makes women into a homogeneous social subject. Throughout all these decades, in Third World countries, women had fought to give decolonial content to women's rights, while simultaneously being subjected to the full force of structural adjustment policies. The International Monetary Fund and the World Bank appropriated the ideology of women's rights as individual rights, and, at the end of the 1970s, the slogan 'women's empowerment' was adopted by the political world, from both the left and the right, from NGOs to feminists of the Global North. For the World Bank, women's empowerment was dependent on policies of both development and of birth rate reduction.[49] For NATO countries, women's rights were integrated into what they claimed were their national values and interest.[50]

The civilizational feminism of the 1980s inherited these ideological frameworks and helped to cement them in place, giving them content. Structural adjustment programs promising development and autonomy took on a female face. Very quickly then, this ploy was mobilized in the service of imperialist campaigns.

While feminism as civilizing mission is not new—it served colonization—by that time, it benefited from exceptional means of dissemination: international assemblies, support from Western and postcolonial states, women's media, economic journals, government and international institutions, grants and support from the World Bank, the International Monetary Fund, foundations, and NGOs. International aid and development institutions made women the pillar of development in the Global South claiming that they were better than men at managing the money they received,[51] that they knew how to save money, and that they complied better with the regulations of the granting programs. In summary, women are good customers, so they will change the world. Women in the Global South have become the custodians of hundreds of development projects—workshops or cooperatives, where the production of local products, like weaving, crafts, and sewing, are valued. Women in the Global North are encouraged to support their 'sisters' of the South by buying their products or by opening up boutiques to sell them, by getting involved in funding and organizing programs to increase their autonomy, their *empowerment* or to teach them management. There are certainly some women in the Global South who have without doubt benefited from these projects, been able to send their kids to school, or risen out of poverty, but these projects can also fail while reinforcing the narcissism of white women who are so happy to 'help' as long as it does not upset their own lives. For the feminist Jules Falquet, 'women's *empowerment*' was set up to respond to the feminization of poverty, in other words, to prop up and perfect policies of pacification and control.[52]

I would like to give an example of the grip of NGO vocabulary in women's groups of the Global South. In March 2018, I was at a meeting in the Northeast of India, attended by about a hundred women from the tribes of Nagaland, a region occupied by the Indian Army. These women experience violence from the army and traffickers, systemic rape, and a high rate of alcoholism and suicide of young men in their communities; they hold their communities on their shoulders. When they presented their actions, they systematically used the language of NGOs: empowerment, capacity building, leadership, governance. They had, one could say, lost their own voices and become custodians of NGO language. I found a way to suggest a critique of this 'language,' inspired by the feminist critique of the ideology of care. I pointed out to them that somehow Western NGOs were condemning them to constant cleansing and to constant repairing of the shattered lives of their communities, while being careful about holding the real perpetrators accountable. Why didn't we spend a little time understanding how their communities had been broken and who had done the breaking? Who was responsible for the hopelessness of the youth? Who was responsible for the rapes and arbitrary arrests? Of course, the women knew the answers to all of these questions, but at first their analyses had been overshadowed by the depoliticizing discourse of NGOs. The latter certainly did face government censorship, but their apolitical discourse was perpetuating the women's oppression. By adopting a gender theory that masks relations of power and political choices, NGOs accepted the narrow path that the Indian government was imposing in the region. My goal here is not to make an easy critique of NGOs, but to study not only how they depoliticize but also how they contribute to new oppressions. The range of pacification techniques is very wide and we must include the 'Girl Power' (women forever remain *girls*) trope of television shows and films. Many of these series, films, and articles are not all bad (I may enjoy some of them), and I do not deny that they can represent important counter-models for little girls, young women, and women, but the massive diffusion of individual stories perpetuates the idea that anyone can fulfill her dream if she is not afraid of challenging certain norms, but never politically. These stories are often based on a psychologization of discrimination. The struggle is rarely collective; the structural cruelty and brutality of power are rarely shown in an explicit way. Heroines are dealing with individuals whose power exceeds their own, but narratives barely touch on what makes up this structure, and how it is based in deep-seated mechanisms of domination and exploitation that have the police, army, court, and state at

The call from Choisir appropriated the arguments of the manifesto on the confinement of Muslim women and the veil as its symbol: "For women, the veil remains the symbol of their confinement and of a Law [sic] that keeps them in inferiority and submission to men."[6] The women who signed this appeal to defend the French form of secularism, came from the historical left, French Resistance fighter Lucie Aubrac, journalist Madeleine Chapsal, director Ariane Mnouchkine, authors Victoria Thérame and Benoîte Groult, and feminist Anne Zelenski, as well as organizations such as the International League against Racism and Anti-Semitism (LICRA), the International Law League of Women (LDIF),[7] the Association of Women Journalists, and the French Movement for Family Planning—a feminist coalition of sorts. There is irony in choosing a space as symbolic as the Mutualité. But it must also be seen as the launching of a work of pacification by appropriating but distorting the history of significant places and of historical figures of struggles for emancipation. War was declared against racialized women, targeting Muslim women in particular, at that November 1989 meeting. This offensive, which began almost 30 years ago and designated Islam as its primary enemy, is still ongoing. The leaders of the LDIF were shocked by what they perceived as the blindness of a left that did not understand that "Koranic education is coupled with medieval practices such as the forced marriage of young, sometimes prepubescent, girls to elderly men."[8] The texts of the LDIF were virulent, mixing denunciations of the Koran, the veil, FGM, and child marriage.[9] These arguments demonstrated the persistence of orientalism, the conviction that 'in our country' (France), 'women are equal to men,' and that therefore, as MP Louise Moreau proclaimed in the November 1989 National Assembly debates, the veil is "a fundamental political problem that affects the status of women, our national identity, and the very future of our national community."[10]

The bicentennial of the French Revolution ironically paved the way for a secular fundamentalism tinged with orientalism. All of the 'language elements' (to speak like those who govern us) of civilizational feminism were put in place: on the one hand, an Islam that imposes women's submission to men and the absolute power of fathers and brothers, and on the other, an equality of the sexes inherent in European culture and the tradition of emancipatory secularism. Patriarchy was no longer a term associated with a global (and thus also European) form of masculine domination; it became consubstantial with Islam. European feminists saw themselves not only as the vanguard of the movement for women's rights but also as their protectors. They presented themselves as the last line of defense against an assault coming from the Global South that threatened all women. At that time, no one could predict what this discourse would bring, nor that it would become the point of convergence between political forces that had previously been hostile to one another.

A Global Offensive against the South(s) and its Gendered Subjects

What emerged in France at the November 1989 meeting was part of a vast global counter-offensive that formed a system comprised of the following: the economic interests of capitalism; programs of structural adjustment, delocalization, and deindustrialization; birth control policies; the reconfiguration of the world after the 1973 oil crisis, the defeat of the US in Vietnam in 1975; and the fall of the Berlin Wall in November 1989. In 1989, as France celebrated the bicentennial of the French Revolution, it welcomed the G7, the meeting of the seven richest countries. The bicentennial ceremonies offered the spectacle of a happy globalization, and, in the context of an ideological revisionism of which historian

François Furet made himself the spokesman, human rights began to replace demands for justice, freedom, and equality. Along the Champs-Élysées, a large night-time parade called 'La Marseillaise'[11] mobilized 6,000 artists and extras to stage twelve living tableaux, each presenting a 'planetary tribe' identified by a 'cultural' symbol: half-naked Africans dancing to the sound of a tam-tam, the British under artificial rain, Soviets marching under paper snow thrown from a truck, white women dressed in basket dresses carrying children from all countries in their arms... At the same time, an event organized at the Mutualité by the International League for the Rights and Liberation of Peoples (which organized the Permanent People's Tribunal) was completely eclipsed by the rejoicing of the G7. The meeting, called the "First Summit of the Seven Poorest Peoples," was based on the "Universal Declaration of the Rights of Peoples" adopted in Algiers in 1976. In 1989, the goal was cancelling Third World debt. The final Declaration, adopted the day after July 14, 1989,[12] was destined for the heads of state of the G7. It affirmed:

It is in agreement with the Universal Declaration of the Rights of Peoples, adopted on July 4, 1976 in Algiers, that we solemnly declare that we contest the right of the 'Big Ones' (*les 'Grands'*) of the earth to confiscate the message of the French Revolution. On this day of celebrating freedom, we consider it hypocritical and even suicidal to speak of justice and wellbeing while the world sinks into ever-deeper inequality and people are marginalized en masse... We denounce the decision-making monopoly of the rich, as a matter of principle, because of its anti-democratic character, but equally because of its concrete consequences. The rich want the system to pick back up and for profit to rebound; they insist that the poor not hinder this 'recovery' even if it aggravates inequality. They argue that the poorest will also benefit in the long run, thanks to the success of the most powerful.[13]

Two discourses and two goals confronted each other: one promising a happy globalization and a harmonious meeting of the 'tribes' of the planet under the aegis of human rights, and the other promising the pursuit of struggle against the North–South axis, against the exploitation of the riches of the South for the wellbeing of the North, and in favor of rights that ensured access to health, education, and land. For the former, celebrations of the French Revolution should contribute to burying once and for all its radical content; for the latter, revolutionary ideas continued to be relevant. An entire European left, and with it, civilizational feminism, jumped headlong into the humanitarian/liberal agenda. Civilizational feminism saw in it the opportunity to finally be admitted into the spheres of power. Their struggle was now cultural and their enemy obvious—Islam. The global configuration offered civilizational feminism the impetus to go along with this counter offensive and gave women's rights a distinctly neoliberal focus.

Enlisting Women in the Civilizing Mission in the Liberal Era

One month before the November Mutualité feminist meeting, on October 24, 1989, the French Movement for Family Planning (MFPF) had published a text that described the veil as a "religious symbol" and "above all a sign of sexist discrimination and a symbol of submission." During the 1970s, feminist and women's groups had developed themes that, despite their shortcomings, evoked the power of emancipation: the denunciation of religious authoritarianism, but not of religion as such; the analysis of sources of discrimination and the mechanism that structures women's domination by

47

the heteropatriarchal order; the connections between capital, the state, and sexism. After the fall of the Berlin Wall, these formulations were caricatured and reduced to invocations of secularism, the dangers of the veil, oppression by Muslim fathers and brothers, etc. Through this regression, civilizational feminism found its place at the heart of the 'new world order.' This transformation of feminism constituted one symptom of 'the end of history.'

The civilizing feminist mission is clear: European women are crusading against sexist discrimination and symbols of submission that persist outside of Western European societies; they present themselves as an army that protects their continent from the invasion of ideas, practices, and men and women threatening their gains. The narrative is obviously false. They needed to depoliticize the struggles of women in the 1970s, dismiss women in the Third World, and erase the contributions of Black feminism. Individual freedom—dressing how I want (with the exception of the veil)—became the (false) symbol of the struggles of the 1970s; it was a clear insult to the struggles of working, immigrant, and refugee women. Civilizational feminism's fight became a universal fight of good against evil. The MFPF continued: "We call on the lucidity of our Muslim sisters who we know are courageous. Courage is shown so often by teenage girls and young women torn between their need for liberation from the male yoke and their desire to remain within their cultural community."[14] This declaration exposes the coloniality of a sisterhood that, besides naturalizing a culture, takes the place of the big sister. This big sister posture recalls the denunciation of the 'fraternalism' of the French Communist Party by Aimé Césaire in his resignation letter to Maurice Thorez in 1956—brother, sure, but big brother. The thousand-year-old submission of Muslim women, secularism as central to women's freedom, Islam as communal straightjacket, 'Muslim culture' or 'Islamic culture' as enemy of girls and young women, Muslim women as potential allies and accomplices in the civilizing feminism mission—all these were becoming widely adopted ideologies by feminist movements, the economic world, the far right, and states.

The November meeting offered arguments to the debates on wearing the veil in school that were taking place at the same time in the French National Assembly. Michèle Barzach, a right-wing MP from Paris and future Health Minister (1986–1988), took them up, in the same colonial terms Fanon described: "Let's win over the women, and the rest will follow." She declared, "Only the women will allow the integration of the Muslim population, since they are the ones breaking down the barriers of tradition and pushing back against the abuse of that tradition where it exists."[15] This argument was immediately repeated by Michèle André, Secretary of State for Women's Rights in the cabinet of socialist Michel Rocard, who himself denounced, in the same breath, forced marriage, FGM, and the submission of "12 to 15 year old" adolescent girls to "the law of fathers and brothers."[16] The law of fathers and brothers (mothers do not exist at all, or only as silent figures subjected to the law of husbands and sons) was naturalized as a cultural fact. Muslim men were said to be harsher, more ruthless, more domineering than any other men. The integration of Muslim women into so-called democratic Western societies was measured by their ability to make these women accept moving away from their families and communities and to participate in their own stigmatization. It was an ideological turning point. By the early 1990s, the World Bank was advocating microcredit to women at the same time that birth control for the South remained central for international organizations. The 1994 Demography Conference in Cairo endorsed both of these practices, and microcredit became the universal solution to women's poverty (which was caused by structural adjustment). Muhummad Yunus, 'father' of microcredit, 'banker of the poor,' received the Nobel Peace Prize in 2006.[17] His 'work' was the basis of a global campaign to empower women through bank loans. Women from the Global South were marked out as easy prey for development policies.

The campaigns, which participated in an ideological offensive against the long history of anti-colonial struggle, were an initiative of the left that had supported them (but often belatedly and half-heartedly). From this moment on, in the eyes of part of the French left, the war for Algerian independence constituted a glorious chapter of its history, while deploring the fact that, having failed to adopt European democracy, the Algerians inevitably condemned women to confinement. That left proclaimed that all struggles for liberation in the South behaved the same way; they had all failed to liberate women. This failure became a central element in feminist parlance, using testimonies from women of the Global South. But by making this strictly the result of a traditional form of patriarchy belonging to the South, positioned against a modern patriarchy of the North, the critique was tweaked and infused with civilizational meaning. All the work of hegemonic feminism from this point forward consisted of demonstrating that this situation was the result of a naïve anti-colonialism. The idea of European superiority thus regained power and the argument according to which these independences were "sending women back to the kitchen" became familiar. Any critique of this position was likened to "cultural relativism." It would have been enough to read decolonial feminist critiques on postcolonial governments to see what a feminist analysis really looks like.[18]

In the early 2000s, civilizational feminism in France, now institutionalized, remained focused on gender discrimination. Women reached managerial positions, thanks to, as the

National Institute of Statistics and Economic Studies (INSEE) itself pointed out:

> the development of service work, which in the past was often confined to the domestic sphere, has been the condition that enabled women's access to the most qualified positions, in enlarging the possibilities of childcare, meals outside the home, etc.... Even as inequalities between the sexes are receding very slowly, new kinds of inequality between women themselves have been added: on the one hand, women who benefit from interesting careers and good salaries, who can reconcile the masculine model of professional success with family life and domestic constraints, and on the other, those who experience precarious employment, forced part-time work, low wages, and who cannot get help in the domestic sphere.[19]

The focus on the veil avoided confronting this contradiction. In 2004, the French Parliament passed a law against wearing the Islamic veil in school, and since then more and more European governments have increased the number of measures and laws targeting Muslim women. The offensive continues against decolonial feminist politics, and throughout Europe, decolonial activists are insulted, threatened, brought before tribunals, accusations of 'anti-white' racism and anti-Semitism are hurled in order to silence decolonial movements and the voices of Black and Muslim women. In two decades, the objectives of civilizational feminism launched in 1989 in Paris have become those of whole governments: the European crusade against Islam stands for the defense of women's rights.

Racialized women have been accepted into the ranks of civilizational feminists on the condition that they adhere to a Western interpretation of women's rights. In the eyes of this ideology, the women of the Global South remain unassimilable because they demonstrate the impossibility of resolving the contradictions produced by imperialism and capitalism through integration, parity, and diversity. Counter-revolutionary feminism thus takes the form of femonationalism, femoimperialism, femofascism, or of marketplace feminism.[20] These feminisms, which do not always share the same arguments or images, find common ground in their adhesion to a civilizing mission that divides the world into cultures open to women's equality and cultures hostile to it.

Following the events in Cologne's central train station on December 31, 2015 (which after inquiry proved that what was presented in the media as Muslim culture and religion's sexist attack against white women was wrong), Alice Schwarzer, a leading figure of German feminism in the 1970s and friend of Simone de Beauvoir, said that from now on, "anti-racism takes precedence over anti-sexism."[21] She denounced "a sort of 'Pavlovian love of foreigners' that is in reality just the other side of hatred of foreigners" and declared, "We do not want to lose our hard-won rights!" For Schwarzer, Muslims threatened the achievements of European feminists. However, Muslims have not been the ones threatening laws about abortion or contraception, nor have they pushed for the exploitation of racialized and migrant women, nor for the systematization of their confinement into part-time, under-paid and under-qualified work. Schwarzer did not hesitate to resurrect the memory of a traumatic event in Germany (the rape of German women by Soviet soldiers, also perpetrated with the same ferocity by American soldiers): "For the first time since the end of World War II, women were victims of organized mass sexual violence in the heart of Europe."[22] In other words, Muslim men in 2015 were the successors of Soviet soldiers who came from a savage and brutal East. "Islamists" are today responsible for rape because they "enjoy turning their frustration and unemployment into feelings of supremacy over the 'infidels' and who

enjoy debasing women."[23] In an interview, Schwarzer demonstrated that French civilizational feminists' argument about
the veil was effectively at the heart of their new civilizing
mission when she wrote that the "veil is the flag and symbol of
Islamists" which "persists as a crusade in the heart of Europe
since the 1980s."[24] Feminist scholar Khola Maryam Hübsch
castigated Schwarzer's Islamophobia, cultural chauvinism,
and the proximity of her views to those of the far right.[25]

Liberal Inclusion

Capitalism has no hesitation in taking up corporate feminism
(which demands integration into its world) or the discourse
of women's rights as long as inequalities between women and
men remain a question of mindset or lack of education rather
than of oppressive structures. Not that the transformation of
mindsets or anti-sexist and anti-racist education are unimport-
ant—far from it—but we must denounce the obstinacy of
not admitting that it is about structures, that without racism,
racial capitalism collapses, and with it, a whole world built on
invisibilization, exploitation, and dispossession. This idea that
we change the world by changing our minds, by learning to
accept difference, is based on an idealist conception of social
relations. But this idea is seductive because it exempts us from
acting on these structures. This is why Chimamanda Ngozi
Adichie's *We Should All Be Feminists* (translated into French
as *Nous somme tous des féministes*) has been such a global
success.[26] The book proposes an inclusive feminism for the
twenty-first century by demonstrating that the gender division
of women/men also impacts men. The norms of heteronormative masculinity are indeed constraining, and becoming a
man often means being subjected to a series of contradictory
and repressive injunctions with respect to feelings, desires,
and bodies. Critique of the virile, militarized, hard body,

which shows no sign of femininity (associated with weakness) reaches a larger audience today, and often intersects with critique of white supremacy and capitalism. The white man (another invention of colonialism) constitutes a powerful tool of racial control, and an analysis of the coloniality of gender cannot afford to lose sight of various masculinities. But there are structural obstacles preventing equality, among women and among men. The inclusive feminism supported by *We Should All Be Feminists* will remain unrealizable as long as all women are not equal, and as long as all men are not equal. So, to which men should women aspire to be equal? Racism and class division, and the two combined, oppose equality. In other words, the argument of *We Should All Be Feminists* is misleading for two reasons. On the one hand, it proposes an idea of inclusive feminism that obscures the entire critique of Black and decolonial feminisms. These latter are precisely tasking themselves with the goal of liberating *all* of society and not 'separating' themselves from men. On the other, such an argument reduces feminism to a simple shift in mindset valid for all women and men, in all places and all times. In her magnificent book, *In the Wake: On Blackness and Being*, Christina Sharpe revisits this thoughtless argument several times, because white, bourgeois feminism has never achieved its own decolonization. Sharpe cites Saidiya Hartman who, in conversation with Frank Wilderson, speaks of "a structural prohibition (rather than merely a willful refusal) against whites being the allies of Blacks due to this species division between what it means to be a subject and what it means to be an object: a structural antagonism."[27]

Femonationalism, Natality, and BUMIDOM[28]

One of the many forms of the North/South structural conflict has been the rise of femonationalism.[29] For Sara Farris, who coined the term and also uses the concept of 'femocratic nationalism,'[30] femonationalism describes the exploitation of feminist concepts by nationalists and Islamophobic neoliberals (who are also often anti-immigration) and the participation of feminists or 'femocrats' in the stigmatization of Muslim men. To analyze this convergence, Farris studies two phenomena: on the one hand, the campaigns for xenophobic and racist policies undertaken in the name of gender equality by far-right political parties in Western Europe; and on the other, the engagement of leading feminists and femocrats in designating Islam as a religion and culture that is inherently misogynistic. These femonationalist campaigns are, according to Farris, inseparable from the reconfiguration of work during the 1980s, especially in the care work industry. To facilitate the entry of migrant and Muslim women into this market, femonationalism developed the following argument: these women, essentially Muslim women, should be saved from the masculine domination whose brutality is inherent in their culture, and their emancipation can only happen if they are encouraged to enter into the neoliberal labor market. The jobs that await them—house cleaners, elder care providers, child minders, or commercial cleaners—are supposed to give them their autonomy and also to allow middle-class European women to enter professional life. White feminists who supported these campaigns found it natural to encourage these women to fill the roles that feminism, at least at one point, had denounced as alienating and as something that masculine domination had reserved for women. They sometimes found allies among racialized women who played the role of native informant, mediator, or translator of neoliberal vocabulary into a language that emphasizes notions of individual choice and freedom. Although we ought not to discount the diversity of destinies among migrant women—their capacity to empower themselves and to escape the injunctions of femonationalism and white feminism—their forced enlistment in the revival of racism and (white) national identities constitutes a major structuring fact. I would like to suggest, however, that the date Farris identifies as the birth of femonationalism—the 2000s in mainland France—should be amended. In effect, femonationalism has been discernable since the 1960s. At that time, a pro-colonial, repressive right wing in the overseas departments and the French government supported youth migration and birth control, while metropolitan society was modernizing. Although feminism in the metropole made some effort to write about the oppression of women in the Antilles,[31] it approached the issue of 'Antillean masculinity' from an angle that psychologized slavery and masculinity. During the 1960s, French society modernized by repressing its colonial past.[32] France needed a feminine workforce to fill lower category positions in the civil workforce: hospitals, nurseries, hospices, kindergartens. White women's greater access to professional life (outside of the factory) required other (racialized) women to take over that social reproduction—childcare, cleaning, cooking—and middle-class families wanted domestic workers. To meet this need, the government created a state institution, the BUMIDOM, which organized young people's emigration from the Antilles, Guyana, and Réunion. Even though in the early years it was mostly aimed at recruiting men, the BUMIDOM quickly began to prioritize women.[33] The organization searched for "candidates for settlement in the metropole and direct placement as domestic workers," indicating that domestic work can be seen as a means for a courageous, young woman to gain a certain degree of instruction, to adapt to metropolitan life in a family unit and to use her free time to expand her knowledge and prepare for exams or courses that would open the door to other professions.[34]

The BUMIDOM emphasized the increase in autonomy and professional experience for Caribbean and Réunionese women. Stéphanie Condon, who has studied French Caribbean women's migration, describes "a concentration of female workers in a small number of sectors, with half of women concentrated in public service industries: hospitals, social services, the post office, sectors where 'feminine' jobs are numerous."[35] Very quickly, the number of Caribbean women recruited by BUMIDOM increased: in 1962, "there were 16,660 Caribbean women in the metropole and 22,080 Caribbean men; in 1968, those numbers were 28,556 and 32,604, respectively. The 1968 census counted 13,736 women and 15,152 men who had moved to the metropole since 1962."[36] Organizing the emigration of a feminine workforce did not only respond to the demand created by the reorganization of capitalism in France, but also to the social and political reorganization of the overseas departments. What I would like to suggest here is that a form of femonationalism emerged in France during a moment of reorganizing its racialized (post) colonial space, once Algeria had become independent. The foundations of the femonationalism of the 2000s were thus laid in the 1960s. The lack of thought given by French feminists to the "postcolonial" moment—in which the repression of the colonial/racial past and reorganization of capitalism are intertwined—is longstanding.

The control of migration, birth control, and the organization of a mobile, racialized, and feminine workforce are at the heart of twenty-first-century neoliberal policies that have been endorsed by civilizational feminists. For example, the Gates Foundation promised to facilitate access to contraceptive information for 120 million women from the poorest countries by 2020 by promoting the distribution of new technologies, in particular hormonal implants (Norplant, Sinoplant, Jadelle), which are inserted into the arm, or hormones that are injected deep into the buttock muscles for a slower release (Depo Provera, Noristerat).[37] The most targeted countries are India,

Nigeria, and Brazil, where the sterilization rate for Black women is high (42%).

The intensification of civilizational feminism was foreseeable. If its first life unfolded during colonial slavery and post-slavery, the postcolonial period in France has revived it. By adopting the fiction that colonialism ended in 1962, feminism deluded itself about both the existence of a vast 'overseas' territory coming out of the slavery and post-slavery period, and the presence within France of racialized women. It thus became an ideology complicit with new forms of capitalism and imperialism, remaining silent on French armed intervention into its former colonies on the African continent as well as on new forms of coloniality and state racism in the overseas departments and in France.

Appropriating the Activist Narrative

Towards the end of the 1980s, one of the ideological weapons of civilizational feminism was the pacification of activists' lives and actions and the rewriting of our struggles. More than the erasure of emancipatory struggles, what mattered to the state, its institutions and its political parties, was rather the integration of some carefully selected figures and their 'whitewashing'—in all senses of that term. This pacification had begun with the activists of 1968, and those who "traded Maoism for the Rotary Club"[38] were now welcomed into the corridors of power. The multifaceted dimension of the Movement for Women's Liberation (MLF)[39] lost its significance. Even though its name was borrowed from movements for decolonization, the MLF soon suppressed its debt to the memories and theories of anti-slavery and anti-colonial movements. The name 'Women's Liberation Movement' was chosen at a time when the term 'feminist' was not hegemonic. For Marxist feminist groups or those close to the anti-imperialist far-left and the Communist Party, the term 'feminist' was associated with a bourgeois position that was blind to the social question; for others, it neglected the question of the unconscious.[40] Other groups defended a political approach of women's struggles, developing a critique of the patriarchal and imperialist state, demonstrating an acute understanding of the social dimension of women's lives; other currents focused more on the denunciation of heteronormativity. Beginning in the second half of the 1970s, more racialized women's groups emerged.[41] Finally, in France as in Italy, there were white feminists who fiercely criticized the focus on legal battles (abortion, contraception, rape), as it meant deferring to the patriarchal state and class-based justice. However, the racial structure of the state, justice, and medicine was still barely called into question. To become a respectable force, a legitimized movement rather than a marginal ideology, civilizational feminism had to transform militant feminism by replacing its previous adversaries (white patriarchy, the state, and capital) with Islam in order to: a) be admitted into the corridors of power, and b) convince the state and capital that a feminism could exist that not only was not a threat, but could potentially be an ideological and political weapon at their service. In France, the MLF, already weakened by the institutionalization of social movements by the socialist government elected in 1981, was reinvented into a feminist movement that demanded parity, aspired to the most banal sexual liberation (while at the same time demanding the repression of sex workers), and made the bikini and miniskirt the symbols of its liberation. This obviously wiped out women's struggles in the factories, queer and lesbian struggles, and the struggles of anti-imperialist feminists, but it was a necessary move in order to magnify a neoliberal ideology that had to distinguish itself from an overly cumbersome patriarchy, especially since at the time it was associated with the conservative right.

This changed feminism rejoiced in re-writing the activist narrative. One of its strategies was to present a radical activist—insulted and defamed in her own time, long without employment because of her activism—as a wise woman, as a shy seamstress with her little bag, who faces the bad guys alone, like Rosa Parks. In this case, the transformation enacted many erasures: of a collective struggle, of the character of the activist, and of the racist structure of the United States. The collective aspect of the struggle, which had been essential to the development of anti-racist politics during the years of segregation in North America, is erased, as for instance the work in 1955, of the Women's Political Council (WPC), which was created to mobilize Black women in the South, and which launched the idea of a boycott of segregated buses. On December 1, 1955, when Rosa Parks refused to sit in the Black section of a bus in Montgomery, the long weeks of boycott that followed were possible thanks to the long preparation undertaken, especially by women. The contribution of the WPC was fundamental to the success of the March on Washington in 1963; WPC activists reserved the bus, prepared the food, printed sheets with the movement songs to prevent boredom on the long journey and to galvanize the protesters; they organized housing in D.C., they were the 'little hands' of the protest, and did the work that women do all the time when it comes to mobilizing on the ground. However, the organizers of the March stubbornly refused to let any WPC members speak during the March on Washington; faced with their objections, it was finally agreed that some of them would be seated in the stands and that a "Tribute to Negro Women Fighters for Freedom" would be organized, even if it would be given by a man, A. Phillip Randolph. Only Daisy Bates, who was a founder of the anti-school segregation movement in Little Rock, Arkansas (which led to the 1954 federal decision declaring desegregation in all schools), was finally authorized to speak.[42] During the March, the Black women organizers were assigned minor roles, behind the men or alongside the wives of male leaders. Not one of them was invited to the meeting with President Johnson. For these women, the "double handicap of race and sex"[43]—the 'Jane Crow' system as Pauli Murray describes it—convinced them that "the Negro woman can no longer postpone or subordinate the fight against discrimination because of sex to the civil rights struggle but must carry on both fights simultaneously."[44] And yet, the contributions of these women still remain marginal in the narrative about the Civil Rights Movement, the hegemonic narrative of which makes the movement into a pacifist rather than peaceful movement and heroizes the individual figure of Rosa Parks, whose militancy is erased. This is how, after a long process of pacification, Rosa Parks can become a figure of North American exceptionalism where mistakes are rectified thanks to the "American values" of *decency* and *fairness*. She enters the American Pantheon on the condition of being 'whitewashed' and separated from her activist community. It is all the more ironic, given that Rosa Parks had been a long-time activist, close to many Black North American communists.[45] Her statue was commissioned by Congress as soon as the whitewashing was complete. It is only once rid of their radical feminism and militancy that women can become figures of national history. What happened to Rosa Parks also happened to Coretta Scott King, who was well known for her opposition to the Vietnam War and her radical activism—she is only remembered as the devoted wife of Martin Luther King, Jr. When the depoliticization of activists is not possible, they are described as viragos, unassimilable extremists, women who are unworthy of their husbands (who themselves become icons), or they are simply doomed to disappear. Among the forgotten or marginalized names that need to be constantly invoked is Claudia Jones: a communist, she proposed a pioneering coordination between the emancipation of women and socialist emancipation and was a cornerstone of the campaign to support the Scottsboro Boys (young Black men falsely accused of rape and threatened with lynching), and had her American citizenship revoked after two stints in prison.[46] One should also mention Winnie Mandela, always negatively compared to her husband who was made a saint by the West (who forget that he was long treated as a terrorist); and Djamila Bouhired.[47] Less assimilable than Djamila Boupacha,[48] because it was impossible to make her into a victim, Bouhired always affirms her pride in having participated in the armed struggle against the French State. The youngest victim of October 17, 1961, was Fatima Bedar, dead at 17 years old.[49]

Temporality and History of Feminism According to the State

Turning an activist into a heroine of Western democracy helps to mask enduring inequalities and makes racism into a disease of the few. Racism and sexism are no longer structural, but accidents to be repaired by the courage of a few individuals. Crime is only a moment of misguidance. This pacification of our militant past contributes to our domination in the present, and power exploits this pacifying narrative to teach contemporary movements a lesson. Norms of respectability are enacted to stifle anger, to make anger dishonorable and fraudulent. There are "subjects worthy of defending and being defended."[50] This strategy of erasure makes these icons—dispossessed of their own struggles and separated from the collectives of which they were members—into calm, gentle, and peaceful heroines. It should be noted that in Europe, it has not yet been necessary to proceed in this way, as no racialized women belong to its Pantheon. And in France, the process of pacifying racialized, militant feminists has not taken place, because their presence would have to be acknowledged in the first place.[51] Black men have been recognized by the French State, but at the price of being whitewashed and having a good part of their activity censored. Hence Aimé Césaire could enter the Pantheon as the author of *Notebook of a Return to a Native Land* but not *Discourse on Colonialism*. The latter denounces racism and proposes an analysis of the boomerang effect of slavery and colonization on France that resonates with our present. In the same way, Frantz Fanon's phrase "I am not the slave of the slavery that dehumanized my ancestors"[52] could be placed at the head of the governmental celebrations of the 150th anniversary of the abolition of slavery in the French colonies in 1998, insofar as all of its revolutionary content was obliterated and the phrase was ripped out of context in order to pronounce a message of reconciliation, without discussing reparations. Should we then desire this entry into their Pantheon, aspire to 'being there,' while the framework of their story has not changed and the place offered remains minor? There is a great temptation to fight for the inclusion of these 'forgotten chapters.' I have myself given in to it, but I quickly saw the limits of this strategy, because if the framework of writing history does not change, it is almost certain that these chapters will only be included at the price of losing their power to transform the world: it will be delimited by the geographical and narrative borders of national history.

Instead of adopting the framework of colonial narratives, which civilizational feminism so cherishes, we must relentlessly recapture the narratives of the struggles of enslaved and maroon women that reveal the existence of an anti-racist and anti-colonial feminism beginning in the sixteenth century. One could object that none of these women called themselves feminists, that the terms anti-racism and anti-colonialism were coined later. But if Mary Wollstonecraft, the philosopher and author of *Vindication of the Rights of Women* (1792), and Olympe de Gouges, author of the *Declaration of the Rights of*

Woman and the Female Citizen, an abolitionist who mounted the scaffold on November 3, 1793 to die for her beliefs, can be called feminists, then so too can Sanité Belair, revolutionary officer of the Haitian Army, shot on October 5, 1802 by the Napoleonic Army during its attempt to re-establish slavery; Queen Nanny in Jamaica; Héva, a maroon in Réunion; and the Mulâtresse Solitude, who participated in the insurrection against Napoleonic troops in Guadeloupe. Rewriting women's history means following the path opened in the United States, in Central and South America, in Africa, in Asia, and in the Arab World, so as to uncover the contributions of Indigenous women, Black women, colonized women, and anti-racist and anti-colonial feminisms.

Solidarity or Loyalty with Racialized Men

Western narratives are not the only ones that erase women in struggle. Revolutionary movements have taken part in the celebration of masculine figures and in making women into silenced heroines. The arguments about division and Occidentalism have been decisive: "you are dividing the movement while it is under the fire of repression, you are participating in the stigmatization of brothers, you are acting like Western women." Many activist women have witnessed how this call to loyalty functions in order to ignore their critique of machismo and sexism. In her autobiography, Elaine Brown, activist and later the leader of the Black Panther Party, bluntly challenges the sexism of her comrades.[53] She describes the spiral of violence created by permanent stress, racism, the terrible repression faced by the BPP, and the capacity of the FBI to sow division.[54] Brown exposes all of the contradictions, all of the terrible tensions that weigh on Black lives, whatever their gender and sexuality, but her observations are made with tenderness and love for the Black women and men who are forced to commit violence against themselves and their loved ones. That is what makes her hard-hitting work so rich and what allows us to interrogate civilizational feminism's moralizing condemnation of masculine domination in Black communities. In France, in their 1978 pamphlet, La Coordination des femmes noires (The Coordination of Black Women) clearly articulated the need for a position separate from both white feminism and Black machismo:

> Coming from a confrontation with our lived experiences as women as much as Black people, we are aware that the history of struggles, in our country and through immigration, is a history in which we are negated, falsified... It is for this reason that our struggle as women is above all autonomous, because in the same way that we intend to fight against the capitalist system that oppresses us, we refuse to suffer the contradictions of activists who, while claiming to fight for a socialism worthy of the name, nevertheless perpetuate in their practice a relationship of domination towards women that they denounce in other contexts.[55]

These positions, traces of which can be found in the texts by enslaved Black women and colonized women, are being taken up today by groups like Locs (Lesbians of Color), Mwasi, and Afro-Fem, who declare that they want to fight "the invisibilization of Black women in feminist movements" without "covering over the machismo of Afro men,"[56] for which they borrowed the concept of "misogynoir" from Moira Bailey. Divine K., co-founder of the Afro-Fem collective, challenges the demand for loyalty by highlighting that "when Black women confront Black men, they are accused of being a source of division, of playing the colonizer's game!" She denounces "the androcentrism of so-called Afro-Consciousness and Afrocentrism movements, which are led by men who promote a sort of 'return to African roots' and impose essentialist requirements on Black women."[57] Solidarity, unfailing solidarity, a love that is real, deep, and unconditional, but which does not tolerate violence, avoids the injunction for loyalty.

Civilizational Feminism as Agent and Pacifier of Women's Struggles

It is important to analyze strategies of pacification because, on the one hand, they do not always follow the path of censorship, policing, or armed repression, and, on the other, because they sow confusion over the objectives of emancipation, representing pacification as a victory of good over evil, of morality over vice. Civilizational feminism has employed these strategies to make the terms 'feminism' and 'feminist' acceptable. It has rewritten the history of women's struggles to undermine or discount the participation and contribution of Global South women in anti-colonial and anti-imperial struggles. Its narrative either mentions them in the margins or accentuates anti-colonial movements' 'betrayal' of these women, who are sent 'back to the home.' This is a deliberate choice: that of ignoring the analyses of women who have participated in anti-colonial and anti-imperialist struggle, who have criticized sexism in nationalism and have insisted on the unavoidable intersections between economic, cultural, political, reproductive, and environmental justice. If a gap exists between the promises of struggles for independence and the postcolonial reality, it is not a matter of culture, but rather of conjecture, which the perpetuation of masculine domination was part of. Contradictions do exist, and, aware of them, decolonial feminists are constantly analyzing them. The hegemonic will of civilizational feminism cannot accept, however, that women of the Global South are able to analyze the mechanisms and ideology of masculinist and heteropa-

66

triarchal politics. In highlighting how the cruelty of white colonialist men has been more globally destructive than any other politics, decolonial feminists do not ignore the existence of systematic violence against women nor the re-emergence of oppressive structures in postcolonial states. Since 2016, the *Ni Una Menos* (Not One [Woman] Less) movement in Argentina has organized strikes and protests against femicide, which they describe as "one of the most extreme forms of violence against women, because it is the murder of a women by a man who considers her as his property."[58] They connect this struggle to the defense of Indigenous peoples' rights to their land and against the neoliberal policies imposed by the IMF.

The Politics of Unveiling in the 2010s

In France, summer is an opportune time for the expression of civilizational feminism and its racist fantasies about the bodies of Muslim women.[59] In summer, a 'woman' *should* undress and not be ashamed of showing her body, because this is how she shows her freedom. Doesn't Marianne, the symbol of the Republic, have one naked breast "because she feeds the people[?] She is not veiled because she is free! This is the Republic!"[60] The bikini[61] has become the iconic clothing of women's liberation, because it symbolizes the victories of "seventies feminists" and incarnates their adherence to "republican values," their access to an authentic and complete, emancipated and fully lived, femininity. Wearing a bikini indicates women's adherence to secularism, since feminism, the Republic, and secularism have become interchangeable. The bikini is the symbol of the opposition to the burkini, which, in the summer of 2016, came to embody the oppression of Muslim women.[62] The burkini was banned by municipal orders, and the police force was ordered to fine women wearing it on the beaches of southern France. The previous year, the summer had seen its share of incidents surrounding women's clothing. The media, social networks, and politicians were obsessed with an incident in Reims, where, according to the local media, four young non-white women had assaulted a young white woman who was sunbathing in a bikini, in a public park. Immediately transformed into an "unacceptable assault of imposing on us a way of life that is not ours" according to one of the leaders of the French right wing calling for "a harsh response,"[63] the Reims bikini affair became, for white feminists on both the right and the left, the occasion to spread accusations of a "religious police"[64] and to praise the nude female body as a symbol of the Republic. By the time an investigation had proven the triviality of the incident, it was too late. The bikini had become a national cause.

The summer of 2017 saw the repetition for what had become a cultural and social norm. At the end of July, the French media spoke daily about a "bikini revolt" in Algeria. The headlines were provocative: "Algeria: The Bikini Revolt Spreads,"[65] "Algeria, What Is This Spontaneous and Citizen Movement of the Bikini Revolt?"[66] French journalists spoke of "feminist protests" of "large, republican protest swims," of assemblies of "over 3,600" women opposing the swimsuit of "Islamists" who "threaten" them.[67] These articles borrowed their vocabulary from a 'secular and republican' feminist rhetoric that hoped to see Algerian women defend "republican values" (i.e. French values) and join in the struggle between "two conflicting visions," modernity or backwardness.[68] Finally, at the beginning of August, corrections began to be made. The Algerian women, who had created a Facebook group to go to the beach together and collectively prevent sexist harassment, challenged the French media so the latter would stop fabricating the "bikini controversy."[69] Nouria, a member of the Facebook group, denounced the manipulation of these terms: "They started using words that we never used, like 'Islamism' and 'obscurantism.'" "We were not denouncing physical aggression, which we did not experience on this beach, nor women wearing the burkini, who never were a problem for us," Sarah, who was also a member of the group, explained further. Her husband Djaffar, exhorted, "Don't think that wearing the bikini or the burkini raise questions for women on the beach. Both have always been there."[70]

The bikini revolt was entirely fabricated by the French media, and white feminists threw themselves right into it. It was, then and always, about unveiling Algerian women, 'so beautiful under their veils,' as the French Army propaganda proclaimed during the war for independence. Feminine beauty depended on unveiling. The ridiculousness of these battles about the bikini should not mask the violence. It is a tactic of imposing norms on non-white women, especially in regard to their clothing.

But the fiction of the bikini revolt was not the last incident of that year's open season on Muslim women. On August 21, 2017, Julia Zborovska published a photo series on her Facebook page of women wearing headscarves, who the media, male and female politicians, and femonationalists call "veiled women."[71] She captioned the photos: "Voilà, an hour spent at the Rivetoile beach in Strasbourg, capital of Europe, the city of human rights... It's clear that it is not the city of women's rights... Liberty, equality between men and women? There are more veiled women than young women in short dresses and skirts... personally I'm shocked to see that. *P.S.* don't bother talking to me about image rights, with their camouflage, no one will recognize them!"[72] Facing accusations of Islamophobia, Zborovska defended herself by invoking her feminism: "I am surprised and a bit shocked by so much hate and anger. I did not mean to provoke this conflict. My message was more feminist than racist. My only regret was not hiding the faces of the women. It was the outfits I wanted to take a picture of. I am anything but racist, fascist, or nationalist."[73] The reference to her feminism, her defensive reaction and her negations—'I did not mean to... I am not racist'—are symptoms of a racist discourse that has nothing to do with individual opinion and everything to do with a structure. Choosing to ignore how racism and Islamophobia insinuate themselves into consciousness, Zborovska could only be surprised by the "hate" and "anger." She could then be oblivious to her own hate. Her message sought to evade guilt: she didn't intend to hurt anyone, why were people hurting her? Continuing to plead innocence, the author played the familiar tune of denial. Caught red-handed, we might say, engaging in Islamophobia, she carried on denying reality by accusing the world of being unjust to her. It is not she who has been unjust and brutal, it was other people. Projection, which has become one of the common tactics of racist discourse—'it wasn't me, it was someone else,' or in translation, 'it's the racialized minorities who are racist, they see evil everywhere'—prevents the subject from having to face her own racism. "Guilt and defensiveness are bricks in a wall against which we all flounder; they serve none of our futures," Audre Lorde has written.[74] But the summer with its abundance of femonationalist declarations was not over. The Lallab association, whose goal is "to make the voices of Muslim women heard in the struggle against racist and sexist oppressions," was told it would no longer receive the help of public service volunteers because they were too close to "indigénistes"[75] and were a "laboratory of Islamism."[76] A petition of support for the organization, "Stop the Islamophobic Cyber-harassment against Lallab,"[77] was immediately accused of encouraging communitarianism by Prime Minister Manuel Valls and Caroline Fourest on Twitter.[78]

The summer of 2017, much like previous summers, was a bolstering season for white feminism and femonationalism, because they found Black and Muslim women on whose bodies their ideology could be deployed. This *dispositif* takes care to reassure public opinion of the cultural superiority of France (by contrasting the freedom of French women to the submission of Black and Muslim women) while disseminating the idea that dark forces are threatening the Republic—and that Muslim women are one of its Trojan horses.[79] Meanwhile, the French media did not write with the same fervor about the women's protests in the Moroccan Rif in July and August 2017 (in support of the Hirak Rif social movement there) or the movements of solidarity initiated by Moroccan Woman in France. Women's struggles for respect and dignity were less important than the 'battle of the bikini' because they would have questioned Islamophobic clichés.

Conservative vs. Liberal Patriarchy

Two forms of patriarchy are clashing right now on the global stage. The first thinks of itself as modern, amenable to a certain kind of multiculturalism, and claims to respect women's rights—so much so that it brings them into the neoliberal economy. It does the same with LGBTQI+ people. The March 2018 opening in Manhattan of Phluid, the first 'gender neutral' store, where "Fashion meets activism", shows that any minoritarian identity can be integrated once it is marketable.[80] Let's be real, the creation of Phluid is not, in itself, a danger to struggle, but Phluid's goal to "empower individuals to be themselves, to express themselves openly, without judgment or fear"[81] fits the individualistic terrain of the market economy.

The other form of patriarchy, masculinist and neo-fascist, directly attacks women and LGBTQI+ people, and aims to reverse hard-won rights—abortion, contraception, the right to work, rights of LGBTQI+ people and especially of trans people. In this system, only women's submission to the heteronormative order, which insists on the absolute power of father and husband, is acceptable. This seismic shift resurfaces in the form of public calls for the rape and murder of feminists, left-wing female politicians, transgender people, queer people, Indigenous women activists, and women migrants. It is a patriarchy that manipulates religion and understands how to stoke hatred and fear, as well as justify murder. The difference between these two patriarchies is in their tone, their ways of speaking and acting, but also in their practice; the neo-fascist patriarchy does not hesitate to use torture, disappearance, prison and death against women, as we can see in the assassinations of Berta Cáceres, an Indigenous environmental activist in Honduras in 2016; of Maria da Lurdes Fernandes Silva, Brazilian land rights activist in 2017; of Mia Manuelita Mascarinas-Green, environmental justice lawyer; of Jennifer López, LGBTQ activist in Mexico; of Sherly Montoya, LGBTQ activist in Honduras; and of Micaela García, feminist activist, in Buenos Aires. In March 2018, the murder of city counselor Marielle Franco and her driver, Anderson Pedro Gomes, in the middle of the street foreshadowed the victory of the extreme-right in Brazil. Masculinist, virilist, patriarchal power allied with neoliberalism did not hesitate to assassinate in public a Black, queer leader of the opposition. The increasing calls for rape on social networks targeting decolonial feminists, queer women, and trans people in India, South America, the United States, and Africa indicate the furor of patriarchy. Everywhere, threats, insults, defamations, sexual harassment, sexual violence, rape, and censorship are used as means of intimidation, as well as calls to order.

We should not let this tension between the two patriarchies blind us, however. The young patriarchs of neoliberalism promise to invite a few women to the front of the line so they may tower over the rest who may survive; the old patriarchs want "their" women to remain silent supporters of their order, want their sons to become patriarchs, and want other women, racialized women, to remain servants and sexual objects in their world.

Politicizing Care

In Europe, Asia, and North America, both communist and anarchist revolutionary experiences—the Paris Commune, the Bolshevik Revolution, the Chinese Revolution, the Cuban Revolution, anarchist communes—have addressed the age-old oppression that housework represents for women. A series of solutions, most often collective ones, have thus been imagined: nurseries open 24/7, collective kitchens, collective housing where housework is distributed in an egalitarian way... Black feminism theorized about this early on, given that Black women have long been assigned the role of domestic servants, caretakers, and cleaners of the white world. During the 1970s, feminist groups in Italy, North America, England, France, and Germany focused on domestic work, especially its unpaid status and, above all, the necessity of considering it as *work*. This Marxist and feminist analysis looked at *work* in the domestic and sex world. In the early 1970s, feminists in Canada founded the Collectif féministe international (CFI) to support the demand of wages for housework. In her 2014 book, Louise Toupin revisits the history of housework struggles led by the CFI and its members' theorization of women's unpaid work.[82] Family and social allowances became struggles in their own right, and, in the United States, the Welfare Movement gave birth to the collective Black Women for Wages for Housework. The Italian feminist Mariarosa Dalla Costa spoke of "the other factory," the social factory, which was to say, the labor of "workers on the street corner" and of "workers in the home" as productive labor, because it produces and reproduces the workforce. In France, Christine Delphy saw in household labor "both one of the most flagrant manifestations of inequality between the sexes which, precisely because of how visible it is, should be easily correctable, and a challenge for equality strategies, as it is also precisely here that activist action finds its limit."[83] The 1970s were a time of intense theorizing and of putting into practice the politics of housework as productive work (with Mariarosa Dalla Costa and Christine Delphy, who have already been mentioned, but also Silvia Federici and Selma James[84]). The analysis of domestic labor inside the family led to "unveiling the extent and invisibility of reproductive labor both private and public, its unpaid status, and the profit that capitalism makes off of it. In sum, it revealed the hidden face of waged society."[85] In 1977, Federici transformed the demand for wages for housework into "a means of concentrating our revolt, a means of organizing ourselves, of coming out of our isolation, of giving a collective, social, international dimension to our struggle."[86] In France, few feminists took note of Françoise Ega's Lettres à une Noire. Récit antillais, which describes the daily life of a Antillean woman domestic worker in France and highlights the racialized character of her work: "We are classified by the government and France in general as being, above all, domestic workers, just as the Polish are agricultural workers, and Algerians are roadworkers."[87] But soon, especially in France, the problem of the division of labor took precedence over the materialist analysis of domestic work. Since then, indifference to the organization of care and cleaning work could only produce white feminist movements' indifference to its growing racialization, while Black feminists in the United States were quick to point out the historical connections between cleaning and care work and racialization. Black feminist chakaZ shows that in applying the notion of alienated labor to gender, race, and sexuality, the entire oppressive character of the system is revealed.[88]

The "Glorious Thirty Years" (1945–1975), a period of French society's enrichment against the backdrop of colonial wars, were notably marked by white, bourgeois women's access to office work. From then on, the demand increased for domestic workers and nannies to look after their homes and children. This female domestic work force was initially drawn from Southern Europe (Portugal) and then from Guadeloupe, Martinique, Réunion Island, and North Africa.

Black feminists have demonstrated that Black women cannot relate to domestic labor in the same way as white women: the racialization of housework has profoundly impacted the issues at stake. Research has been made on the differences between female domestic workers (based on where they come from, whether or not they live with their employers, and whether they have to care for children or the elderly) as well as the state-based solutions of various countries. And despite the difficulties of organizing themselves, domestic workers have overcome loneliness and isolation to find ways of collectively organizing, of making their working conditions, and the exploitation to which they are subjected, visible.

Wearing Out[89] *the Body or Exhausting Racialized Bodies*

In what follows, I would like to dwell on some of the points I raised in the introduction: the economy of wearing out and tiring out racialized bodies. The anthropologist David Graeber has spoken of the need to reimagine the working class as what he calls "the caring class," the social class where "work is about taking care of other humans, plants, and animals."[90] He proposed the following definition of care work: "work in which the goal is maintaining or expanding the freedom of another person." Or "the more your work helps others, the less you get paid to do it."[91] We must, he says, "rethink the working class by putting women first, contrary to the historical representation we have of workers."[92] I propose going even further in focusing on the economy of using and using up of racialized bodies, cleaning as practice of care, and the instrumentalization of the separation of clean/dirty in the gentrification and militarization of cities.

I am referring here to an economy that *wears out* racialized bodies, depletes the strength of certain individuals designated by capital and by the state as fit to be used up, to become victims of illnesses, debilitations and disabilities that, even though they may be recognized by the state after bitter struggles, are never used to challenge the very structure that causes them. Wear and tear on the body (which of course concerns men also, but I insist on the feminization of the cleaning industry) is inseparable from an economy that divides bodies between those who have a right to good health and to relax, and those whose health does not matter and who do not have the right to rest. The economy of exhaustion, of fatigue, of wearing out gendered and racialized bodies, is constant in the testimonies of women who work in the cleaning industry. Fernande Bagou, who was one of the spokespersons for the January 2018 strike of women cleaners at the Gare du Nord, explains that she gets up at 4:00 a.m., takes a bus at 5:30 in order to catch a train, then another, in order to be at work by 7:00 a.m.[93] She picks up her supplies and begins to clean the station, inside and out. Then, she takes a train to another station:

We sweep, we pick up the trash, which is heavy, and we do it without a cart. It is up to us to carry it. We repeat the same movements. Walking weakens the ankles and the knees; our wrists are also affected. With this job, it hurts to walk normally. It hurts all over.[94]

In Maputo, Camarada Albertina Mundlovo has to arrive at work before her employers. Terrified of arriving late, she catches a public taxi in the opposite direction and then doubles back towards the city: "I end up paying double, but if I waited for a direct route, I would never get on. Women have lost their lives fighting for a spot. Employers do not want to hear about our difficulties."[95] Whether in the United States, Europe, Asia, South America, or Africa, if you go out early in the morning, you will encounter sleepy women in transit or rushing to work before the city wakes up.

Capitalism is an economy of waste, and this waste must disappear before the eyes of those who are entitled to enjoy a good life: it must be disposed of without being seen. According to the World Bank, the global production of material waste rose in 2016 to 1.3 billion tons per year, about 11 million tons per day. Obviously, not all of this waste is cleaned by women, but also by men and children who clean mountains of household and toxic waste—garbage collectors, Dalits who empty the sewers, Africans who dismantle technology waste in Accra, the workers who unload ships in Bangladesh, etc. I want to highlight here that this economy of waste production is inextricably linked to the production of human beings as 'scum,' as 'waste.' An entire humanity is condemned to undertake invisible and overexploited work to create a world suitable for hyper-consumption and maintaining institutions. For those people: the dirt, the pollution, the non-potable water, the uncollected garbage, the plastics that invade everything, the gardens where plants die from lack of maintenance, the sewers that do not work, the polluted air. For others: the clean city, the gardens, the flowers, the serene wandering. The world is segregated through a division of the clean and the dirty, which rests on a racial division of urban space and the environment, a division that also exists in the Global South. Among the racialized people condemned to cleaning the bourgeois world,

I focus on women housekeepers, called 'surface technicians (*techniciennes de surface*)' in France, who, here as elsewhere, lead crucial struggles: they reveal the structural and unequal character of the feminized and racialized cleaning industry, as well as its connection to a slave and colonial past.

Cleaning is becoming a more and more dangerous industry because, in addition to muscular-skeletal disorders,[96] the chemical risks are growing because of the composition of the products that are used.[97] Harassment and sexual violence are integral parts of this industry of precariousness and exploitation; they indicate that the abuse of power is structural, that it is not a simple expression of an 'abnormal' masculinity, but is inscribed in the very fabric of this industry. The care/cleaning industry is one of the clearest examples of how racial capitalism functions through the production of vulnerability to premature death, as Ruth Wilson Gilmore has explained. In effect, this industry exposes racialized women to toxic products, sexual harassment and violence, invisibilization, exploitation, the organization of both legalized and criminalized immigration, and the denial of rights.

Who Cleans the World?

In France, housework was industrialized in the nineteenth century, first with women from the working classes or the countryside, then with enslaved and colonized women. During the 1960s, outsourcing this activity created new categories of work (which became legally institutionalized under French labor law as 'socio-economic and professional categories' under the 1981 reforms). According to the Federation of Cleaning Businesses and Associated Services (Fédération des entreprises de la propreté et services associés), the cleaning industry in France is in a state of constant expansion (currently one of every 40 workers in France). It represents an annual revenue of 13 billion Euros, employs 500,000 people of which two-thirds are women, and of which 50% are over 44 years old. In 2004, 29% of people employed in this industry were foreign nationals and 76% worked in Île-de-France.[98] Part-time work predominates (79%) in the industry; 47% of employees work for multiple agencies, and women are the majority of service workers, though men are more often in supervisory positions. L'Observatoire de la propreté explains that part-time employment is offered to employees to adapt to the needs of women.[99] Primary clients are offices (38%), followed by hotels (19%) and manufacturing (13%).[100] All of this shows the structuring character of racialization, feminization and precariousness to cleaning work and highlights the importance of this sector in service-based economies and in our gentrified metropolises.

In France, the family company Onet, founded in 1860 (whose descendants have remained in charge of the company), dominates the market. As soon as the SNCF was set up in the nineteenth century, Onet secured an exclusive contract for cleaning both the stations and the trains.[101] The company has expanded into the fields of security (mostly men), nuclear waste management, logistical services, and care for the elderly. On Onet's website, the company's chief values are said to be "Listening, Respect, Boldness." The site informs the public of the creation of the Onet Foundation, whose "mission is to support action in favor of solidarity and the struggle against substandard housing by participating in concrete actions on the ground and by promoting awareness of the problem." Onet supported the release of Al Gore's film on climate as well as the ecological film *Tomorrow*. The company claims to adhere to the ten principles of the United Nations Global Compact on Sustainable Development, and respect for social dialogue, and engagement in the "development of employability." It has a service, Oasis Diversité, that runs training sessions in cleaning, technology, and hospitality professions.

Between 2008 and 2016, its revenue increased from 1.3 billion Euros to 1.741 billion, half of which is due to the increase in Onet Services Network professions, which grew by more than 5%.[102] Employees are "partners," who are invited to progress, thanks to the "Onet University." In 2016, Onet had "64,392 partners," (i.e., workers) 63% of whom were women. In the professions of the Onet Services Network, there is "an important difference between the cleaning professions, where the majority of workers are female, and the security professions, where the situation is the opposite."[103] In other words, by the company's own admission, and despite all the examples of managerial hypocrisy mentioned above, it is racialized women who do the cleaning. An entire series of video clips promoting Onet is available on YouTube.

One clip entitled "Life Is Beautiful" (*La vie est belle*, 2016) is telling. The title echoes Roberto Benigni's film, in which a father lies to his son in order to hide the horrors of the Nazi concentration camp to which they are deported, and though I do not know if the analogy between the Benigni film and the clip was intentional, the alignment of the two narratives does not lack irony. In the Onet clip, a blond woman in a pantsuit is seen entering an office, smiling. Around her, women and men are cleaning walls, floors, and cabinets, but they are invisible to her, she does not see them. She then goes to the supermarket, where, thanks to Onet, the things she buys are clean and hygienic. She takes a train cleaned by Onet before going to a stadium cleaned by Onet and visiting someone in a hospital cleaned by Onet. Finally, she enters a hotel room that has just been cleaned by an Onet employee. At the end of the clip, she is seen walking on a lawn cleared of trash by Onet.[104] Throughout the clip, the invisibility of the people doing the work is foregrounded. White women can be assured of finding everything clean, but without confronting the reality of who is doing the cleaning, and therefore of the presence and existence of those who do it. This is one of the fundamental principles of cleaning: it must remain *invisible*. Through this invisibilization, the person doing the cleaning disappears not only from the screen, but the violence and disdain they encounter on the job are legitimized. One only has to contrast this video with the interview with Madame Gueffar, brutally fired by Onet after working for them as a cleaner at the Agen Train Station for 14 years, without missing a single day.[105] Cleanliness is based on violence and arbitrariness. But *the wealthy white woman*, who lives in a clean and secure world thanks to *racialized women* (and men, for the security), should see neither these women nor the violence. However, the clip "Life Is Beautiful" contains another element: the employees it shows are overwhelmingly white. Doubtless, a clip that showed the real proportion of racialized people in these occupations would have exposed too blatantly their gendered racialization.

This brings me to the question that I would like to put at the heart of decolonial feminism: who cleans the world? How can we understand the relationship between capitalism as material and toxic waste producer, and its production of human beings seen as disposable? How is the outsourcing of waste invisibilized? How do we put our solidarity with care workers and cleaning workers into practice? In March 2018 in Chennai, Dalit curator Krishnapriya opened her exhibition "Archiving Labor" whose venue, the College of Fine Arts, was originally a colonial technical school. In this exciting exhibition of 30 young Dalit artists, one particular installation caught my eye because it dealt with cleaning work. It consisted of multiple portraits of the women who clean the Chennai train stations and of their activities, in which they are seen, for instance, removing human excrement from the rails and trains. A young artist added three notebook pages on which he handwrote the following words: "Cleaning feces is not a normal thing. With his bare hands, my grandfather cleaned human feces to the point that it filled the lines on his hands, like blood on blood." He concluded, "This woman should stop cleaning human excrement; everyone should clean their own excrement. We should join this woman in cleaning human excrement, that way, this woman would become our equal, and she would become our equal concretely, not just in words."[106]

In many countries, workers in the cleaning industry are organizing themselves, and some have done so for many decades, demanding the recognition of their rights, social protection, an end to harassment and sexual violence, as well as systematic precariousness. One concept comes up again and again: dignity. By forcefully affirming that they do their jobs well, that they like their job, cleaning workers insist on the dignity and respect they are entitled to. Their fight is at the heart of feminist struggles for dignity, against racism, and against exploitation. The age-old work of women—'cleaning' work—is indispensable to the perpetuation of patriarchal and capitalist society, and in France, we must integrate into its history the care and cleaning work assigned to Black women slaves and domestic workers, then to colonized women, and today to racialized women of both French and foreign origin. The struggles of racialized cleaning women give new content to 'women's rights.' They articulate what the right to exist can mean in a world where rights were designed to exclude. For decolonial feminists, the analysis of cleaning and care work in the contemporary configuration of racial capitalism and civilizational feminism is the most urgent task.

Reconnecting with the Feminist Power of Imagination

The idea that women do not have a past, and do not have a history, means, of course, that they have one but that it has been buried, hidden, and masked, and that the job of feminists has been to find it and make it known. This work of archeology, of rediscovery, of appropriation is ongoing and fundamental. However, by reversing the meaning of this phrase, in affirming that we have a history and past, I am suggesting a different approach to writing this history. I question the meaning of this "past" and this "history" in the slogan of the women's rights movement: "We who are without a past, women / we who do not have a history." In what way does it help us to transform the catastrophic inheritance of the history of racialized peoples (slavery, genocide, dispossession, exploitation, deportation) into a narrative? How can we write the past and history of these catastrophes that we hardly ever mention? What words can we find to speak of the general offensive all over the world that "tends to make habitable and still inhabited lands disappear to turn them into links in the global chains of production-consumption" when "zones of sacrifice are multiplied"?[107] Where is the sense in declaring that "women" have no past and no history while, among women, white women and racialized women are in no way given the same legitimacy? Writing the past and the history of racialized women has not had the same trajectory as European feminist writing because it has not followed the same process. For racialized women, it is not about filling a void, but about finding the words to breathe life into that which has been condemned to non-existence, worlds that have been cast out of humanity.

In conclusion, I leave you with the words of a text written collectively in June 2017, in which 30 of us artists and activists wrote, "We want to implement utopian thinking, intended as an uplifting energy and force, as a presence and as an invitation to emancipatory dreams, and as a gesture of rupture: to dare to think beyond that which is presented as 'natural,' 'pragmatic,' or 'reasonable.' We do not want to construct a utopian community but to return all of its creative force to dreams of defiance and resistance, justice and freedom, happiness and kindness, friendship and wonder."[108]

Notes

Preface

1. "Feminist racism" was coined by Sabine Hark and Paula-Irene Villa in *The Future of Difference. Beyond the Toxic Entanglement of Racism, Sexism and Feminism*. Translated form German by Sophie Lewis. Verso, 2020, p. xi.

2. Verónica Gago, *Feminist International. How to Change Everything*. Translated form Spanish by Liz Mason Deese, Verso, 2020, p. 3.

3. Frantz Fanon, "Algeria Unveiled" in *A Dying Colonialism*, translated from the French by Haakon Chevalier, Grove Press, 1965, p. 37.

4. Fred Magdoff and Chris Williams, "Capitalist Economies Create Waste, Not Social Value," *Truthout*, August 17, 2017, p. 19. See also Susan George, "Waste and Capitalism," January 17, 2011, www.tni.org/en/article/waste-and-capitalism; Simonetta Falasca-Zamponi, "Waste and Consumption: Capitalism, the Environment and the Life of Things," August, 2012; Françoise Vergès, "Capitalocene, Waste, Race and Gender", e-flux, #100, 2019, www.e-flux.com/journal/100/269165/capitalocene-waste-race-and-gender/ and "Racial Capitalocene" in Gaye Theresa Johnson and Alex Lubin, eds, *The Future of Black Radicalism*, Verso, 2017.

5. Françoise Vergès, *The Wombs of Women. Race, Capitalism, Feminism*. Duke University Press, 2020.

6. Gago, *Feminist International*, p. 17.

Translator's Introduction

1. María Lugones, "Heterosexualism and the Colonial / Modern Gender System," *Hypatia* 22, no. 1 (2007): 186–209.

2. Sara Farris, *In the Name of Women's Rights: The Rise of Femonationalism* (Durham: Duke University Press, 2017); Puar, *Terrorist*

Assemblages: Homonationalism in Queer Times (Durham: Duke University Press Books, 2007).

3. Angela Y. Davis and Cornel West, *Freedom Is a Constant Struggle: Ferguson, Palestine, and the Foundations of a Movement*, ed. Frank Barat (Chicago: Haymarket Books, 2016).

4. Ashley J. Bohrer, *Marxism and Intersectionality: Race, Class, Gender, and Sexuality under Contemporary Capitalism* (Berlin: Transcript Verlag, 2019).

5. Audre Lorde, "Age, Race, Class, and Sex: Women Redefining Difference," in *Sister/Outsider* (Berkeley: Crossing, 1983).

Introduction: Invisible, They "Open the City"

1. Frantz Fanon, *A Dying Colonialism*, trans. Haakon Chevalier. New York: Grove Press, 1994, p. 37.

2. Audre Lorde, "The Uses of Anger: Women Responding to Racism," in *Sister/Outsider: Essays and Speeches*. New York: Ten Speed Press, 2007, pp. 124–33.

3. In *L'idéologie raciste* (1972), sociologist Colette Guillaumin proposed the notion of *racisation* to describe the processes by which power assigns non-white individuals to subaltern positions and justifies racial discriminations. "No, race does not exist. Yes, the race does exist. No, of course, she is not what they say she is, but she is nonetheless the most tangible, real, brutal, of realities," Guillaumin wrote in, *Sexe, race et pratique du pouvoir: L'idée de nature*, Paris: iXe, 2016, p. 140. *Racisé·e·s, racialisé·e·s* ("racialized") was adopted by anti-racist movements in the early 2000s to speak of Black, Maghrebin, Asian, Muslim, and Indigenous women and men to denounce systemic, structural racism.

4. The SNCF is France's state-owned national railway company. The Gare du Nord is one of six major SNCF stations in Paris and the busiest railway station in Europe. —Trans.

5. The original statement, "We defend the right to hit on people as fundamental to sexual liberation" can be accessed here: www.lemonde.fr/idees/article/2018/01/09/nous-defendons-une-liberte-d-importuner-indispensable-a-la-liberte-sexuelle_5239134_3232.html (accessed January 2, 2021). A partial English translation of the statement ran here: www.deadline.com/2018/01/catherine-

deneuve-defends-men-sexual-harassment-1202239110/ (accessed January 2, 2021). —Trans.

6. Literally meaning "denounce your pig," the hashtag is roughly the French version of #MeToo, though the latter is also used in France. It was started in October 2017 by Sandra Muller, a French journalist who lives in New York. —Trans.

Chapter 1   Taking Sides: Decolonial Feminism

1. I summarize below Sara Farris' analysis of these points of convergence in Sara Farris, *In the Name of Women's Rights: The Rise of Femonationalism*. Durham: Duke University Press, 2017.

2. Angela Y. Davis and Cornel West, *Freedom Is a Constant Struggle: Ferguson, Palestine, and the Foundations of a Movement*, ed. Frank Barat. Chicago: Haymarket Books, 2016, p. 137.

3. E. P. Thompson, *The Making of the English Working Class*. New York: Vintage, 1966, p. 12.

4. The University of Feminism was organized by Marlène Schiappa, the French State's Secretary of Equality between Women and Men from 2017 to 2020 in the first government of Emmanuel Macron. The event took place in Paris on September 13-14, 2018. Schiappa said of the University:

> Our desire was to highlight the plurality of feminist movements because the movement has never been monolithic; it has always been crossed by different currents. We wanted to have a place of debate anchored in three watchwords: reflections, opinions, and actions. It is a central concern of President Emmanuel Macron's five-year term to make sure these debates permeate society.

5. Réunion Island is one of five departments of the French State outside of Europe; it became a department in 1946 after hundreds of years of French colonial occupation. Réunion Island is located in the Indian Ocean between Madagascar and Mauritius. —Trans.

6. As Vergès gives context to this Ordinance elsewhere:

> The decree was originally a clause of a February 4, 1960 law enacted by [Michel] Debré's government to deal with opposition to the Algerian War. The decree authorized the French government to take 'all necessary measures to maintain order,

safeguard the State and the Constitution, and pursue the pacification and administration of Algeria.' It was a decree enacted against French civil servants living in Algeria who supported the Algerian nationalist struggle.

Françoise Vergès, *Monsters and Revolutionaries: Colonial Family Romance and Metissage*. Durham: Duke University Press, 1999, p. 116n76. —Trans.

7. Prosper Ève, *Île à peur. La peur redoutée ou récupérée à la Réunion des origines à nos jours*. Saint-André, Réunion: Océan Éditions, 1992.

8. Frantz Fanon, *The Wretched of the Earth*, trans. Richard Philcox, reprint edition. New York: Grove Press, 2005, p. 58. Translation modified.

9. France is administratively divided into various departments (currently, 96 in Europe and five overseas). In 1947, the French Constitution redefined five of its previous colonies into departments of France, with the same legal status as any of the other regions of France. This included French Guiana, Guadeloupe, Martinique, Réunion, and Mayotte. Collectively, they are referred to as the *département et régions d'outre-mer* or abbreviated as *DROM*. —Trans.

10. In what follows, I use either "a movement" or "movements" in order to avoid saying "the movement." I do so in order to signal a plurality of feminisms, the possibility of alternative forms of these feminist alternatives. But all of these are resolutely anti-racist, anti-capitalist, and anti-imperialist, which is what interests me here.

11. In France, the term "Negrophobia" to describe anti-Black racism emerged with the creation in 2010 of the Anti-Negrophobia Brigade, which denounces state racism and advocates political anti-racism. See www.facebook.com/BrigadeAntiNegrophobiePageOfficielle/ (accessed July 2018).

12. Cited in Sabelo J. Ndlovu-Gatsheni, *Epistemic Freedom in Africa: Deprovincialisation and Decolonization*. London: Routledge, 2018, p. 64. The cited piece can be found here: Peter P. Ekeh, *Colonialism and Social Structure*. Ibadan, Nigeria: University of Ibadan, 1983.

13. *Marronnage*: running away from the plantation for a day, a month, or years. Maroons carved territories of freedom in the lands of

unfreedom in the Caribbean, Indian Ocean, and American colonies. They fought against the militia and armies sent by colonial powers, forcing them in some cases to sign treaties recognizing their sovereignty (the names *quilombos* in Brazil or *palenques* in South America resonate to this day). They preserved rituals, language, and cultures. Their names and practices of resistance, which are in popular memories synonyms of struggles against racism and colonialism, are being reappropriated to design current strategies of resistance.

14. Aimé Césaire, *Discourse on Colonialism*. New York: Monthly Review Press, 1973, p. 35.

15. This quote is taken from Lilla Watson's speech at the 1985 United Nations' World Conference on Women in Nairobi that culminated in the United Nations Decade for Women. But Watson prefers to say that the sentence is the result of a collective reflection of Aboriginal activist groups in Queensland in the 1970s.

16. Darren Lenard Hutchinson, "Identity Crisis: 'Intersectionality,' 'Multidimensionality,' and the Development of an Adequate Theory of Subordination," *Michigan Journal of Race and Law*, 2001, vol. 6, pp. 285–317, p. 309.

17. Félix Boggio Éwanjé-Épée, Stella Magliani-Belkacem, Morgane Merteuil, and Fréderic Monferrand, "Programme pour un féminisme de la totalité" in Tithi Bhattacharya et al., *Pour un féminisme de la totalité*, Paris: Éditions Amsterdam, 2017, pp. 13–31, p. 18.

18. Ibid, p. 23.

19. Françoise Vergès, *The Wombs of Women: Race, Capital, Feminism*, trans. Kaiama L. Glover. Durham: Duke University Press, 2020.

20. The presentation was made in countries of the Global South during conferences and workshops about decolonial pedagogies. An article developed from this presentation: Françoise Vergès, "Bananes, esclavage et capitalisme racial," *Le Journal des Laboratoires d'Aubervilliers, Cahiers C*, 19, 2018–2019, pp. 9–11.

21. Elsa Dorlin, *La matrice de la race: généalogie sexuelle et coloniale de la nation française*. Paris: La Découverte, 2006.

22. Gloria Wekker, *White Innocence: Paradoxes of Colonialism and Race*. Durham: Duke University Press, 2016.

23. Fatima El-Tayeb, *European Others*. Durham: Duke University Press, 2011, p. xv.

24. Reni Eddo-Lodge, *Why I'm No Longer Talking to White People About Race*, London: Bloomsbury, 2017.

25. Elsa Dorlin, *La matrice de la race: généalogie sexuelle et coloniale de la nation française*. Paris: La Découverte, 2006.

26. For more on this, see Boaventura de Souza Santos, *Epistemologies of the South: Justice Against Epistemicide*. London: Routledge, 2014.

27. The term Vergès uses here—'minoration'—has both the sense of devaluation and the sense of placing someone in the (legally and culturally) inferior or dependent position of children. —Trans.

28. María Lugones, "Heterosexualism and the Colonial/Modern Gender System," *Hypatia*, 2007, vol. 22, no.1, pp. 186–219; Lugones, "Colonialidad y género," *Tabula Rasa*, no. 9, 2008, pp. 73–101. In French, this theory is taken up in Jules Falquet's introduction to the text "Les racines féministes et lesbiennes autonomes de la proposition décoloniale d'Abya Yala," *Contretemps*, April 2017, in two parts.

29. Oyèrónké Oyěwùmí, *The Invention of Women: Making an African Sense of Western Gender Discourses*. Minneapolis: University of Minnesota Press, 1997.

30. For more on the politics of pity and French abolitionism, see Françoise Vergès, *Abolir l'esclavage, une utopie coloniale. Les ambiguïtés d'une politique humanitaire*. Paris: Albin Michel, 2001.

31. Most contemporary English-language translations title the play *Black Slavery*, but de Gouges' French term 'nègres' more accurately corresponds to the English 'negro' or 'nigger,' depending on context —Trans.

32. On the critics of Olympe de Gouges' play, see Tomasz Wysłobocki, "Olympe de Gouges à la Comédie-Française: un naufrage dramatique," *Fabula / Les colloques*, Théâtre et scandale (I), URL: http://www.fabula.org/colloques/document5884.php (accessed December 29, 2020); Blanc, Olivier, "Une humaniste au XVIIIe siècle: Olympe de Gouges," ed. Évelyne Morin-Rotureau, *Combats de femmes 1789–1799. La Révolution exclut les citoyennes*. Paris: Autrement, 2003, pp. 15–33; René Tarin. "*L'Esclavage des noirs*, ou la mauvaise conscience d'Olympe de Gouges," *Dix-huitième*

Siècle, *La recherche aujourd'hui, sous la direction de Michel Delon*, 1998, no. 30, pp. 373–81 (all accessed July 2018).

33. The film *Indochine* (Régis Wargnier, 1992) is a good example of this filmwashing. It is about a white French woman, Éliane Devire, who in the 1930s directs a rubber tree plantation with her father Émile. Described as being fair to her workers (though most rubber plantation used forced labor), she adopts Camille, an orphan princess from Annam (the French protectorate in Central Vietnam). They both fall in love with a young officer in the French navy, and what follows is more of the same: colonial nostalgia accompanied by a watered-down version of the anti-colonial struggle.

34. The baccalaureate is a set of exams that French students take at the end of secondary school; passing is necessary in order to work in certain professions, to enter university, or to be eligible for certain forms of further professional training. —Trans.

35. Fanny Gallot, "Le 'travail femme' quotidien de 'Revo,' puis de l'OCT dans les entreprises (1973–1979)" in *"Prolétaires de tous les pays, qui lave vos chaussettes?" Le genre de l'engagement dans les années 1968*, eds. Ludivine Bantigny, Fanny Bugnon, and Fanny Gallot. Rennes: PUR, 2017, pp. 109–22, p. 119.

36. The current French government promises African women access to modernity thanks to their adoption of the French language, all while resorting to colonial arguments about African women's birth rate, casting them as responsible for poverty on the continent. Emmanuel Macron said of African women on July 8, 2017: "When today, countries are still having 7–8 children per woman, you can decide to spend billions of Euros, but you will still not stabilize anything."

37. Auclert transformed the original quote which read "this slave according to reality is the woman" (*cette esclave selon la réalité, c'est la femme*). Letter of Victor Hugo to Léon Richter (director, with the feminist Maria Deraismes, of the journal *L'Avenir des femmes*), *Écrits politiques, Anthologie établie et annotée par Franck Laurent*. Paris: Le livre de poche, 2001, cited in https://www.huffingtonpost.fr/morgane-ortin/lettre-de-victor-hugo-a-leon-richer_b_9391064.html (accessed December 26, 2020).

38. Conference by Edith Taïeb, "Hubertine Auclert: 'de la République dans le ménage' à la 'vraie République'," Abbaye St Vincent, Le Mans, November 3, 2003, https://www.pedagogie.ac-nantes.fr/ histoire-geographie-citoyennete/ressources/hubertine-auclert-de-la-republique-dans-le-menage-a-la-vraie-republique-599669. kjsp (accessed October 14, 2018). In her work, *Arab Women in Algeria* (trans. Jacqueline Grenez. Brovender: De Gruyter, 2014), Auclert advocates for colonial assimilation over a colonialism of contempt and the cruelty of civil servants. She wrote that 'Arabs' wanted assimilation and that the dream of Muslim women was to be like French women. This orientalist text brings together the elements of colonial civilizational feminism: some ethnography and tourist sociology, clichés about the 'resigned' character of the Arabs, polygamy, and 'Arab marriage' that is really 'child rape.' For Auclert, French women who were, because of their condition, close to Arabs were best positioned to study them.

39. Klejman and Rochefort's presentation does not address feminists' attitudes towards racism and colonialism, continuing the dominant tradition in French research of ignoring the role of the colony in the field of politics. Laurence Klejman and Florence Rochefort, "Le féminisme, une utopie républicane 1860–1914," presented at the conference "Femmes et pouvoirs, XIXe-XXe siècle" in 2018. www.senat.fr/colloque_femmes_pouvoir (accessed July 2018).

40. Hubertine Auclert, "Les femmes sont les n...," in *Le Vote des femmes*. Paris: V. Giard & E. Brière, 1908, pp. 196–8.

41. Frantz Fanon, "Algeria Unveiled," in *Decolonization: Perspectives from Now and Then*, ed. Prasenjit Duara. London and New York: Routledge, 2003, pp. 42–55, p. 44.

42. In 1945, Aimé Césaire painted a very negative picture of the centuries of French colonization at the Constituent Assembly: no schools, high mortality rate, the economy in the hands of a few, etc. In 1954, in Algeria, 10% of the population (of which a large majority were settlers) held 90% of the country's wealth. For 200,000 European children, there were 11,400 schools, while 1,250,000 Arab and Berber children shared 699 institutions. On the eve of independence in the 1950s, only 4% of school-age girls went to school (10% of all Algerian children and 97% of European children), even though a "schooling plan" had been passed by decree on November 27, 1944.

The few training centers that did open, in particularly during the Centenary of 1930, confined young women and girls to learning household tasks (cooking, ironing) or crafts (carpet weaving, embroidery, etc.) and in any case, their enrollment numbers were so low as to be purely symbolic. See: Feriel Lalami, "L'enjeu du statut des femmes durant la période coloniale en Algérie," *Nouvelles Questions féministes*, 2008/3, vol. 27, pp. 16–27. DOI: 10.3917/nqf.273.0016. URL: www.cairn.info/revue-nouvelles- questions-feministes-2008–3-page-16.htm (accessed July 2018).

43. National Security Memorandum, *Implications of Worldwide Population Growth for U.S. Security and Overseas Interests*, December 10, 1974, declassified in March 1989.

44. See Françoise Vergès, *The Wombs of Women: Race, Capital, Feminism*, trans. Kaiama L. Glover. Durham: Duke University Press, 2020.

45. www.un.org/fr/sections/issues-depth/women (accessed July 2018).

46. "World Wide Status and Rights of Women: Telegram of the Department of State to All Diplomatic and Consular Posts," May 31, 1979. www.history.state.gov/historicaldocuments/frus1977–80v02/d327 (accessed July 2018). On the impact of the international politics of the 1970s on feminism see Karen Garner, "Global Gender Policies in the Nineties," *Journal of Women's History*, vol. 24, no. 4, 2012; Susan Watkins, "Which Feminisms", *New Left Review*, Jan–Feb 2018, no. 109, pp. 5–72.

47. Jules Falquet's work on the Decade for Women, the international politics of gender and its consequences on the politics of development for women in the Global South is clarifying. See: "Penser la mondialisation dans une perspective féministe," in *Travail, Genre, Société*, 2011, vol. 1, pp. 81–98; "L'ONU, alliée des femmes? Une analyse féministe du système des organisations internationales,", *Multitudes*, January 11, 2003, pp. 171–91.

48. See Jules Falquet, *Multitudes*, Ibid.; Greta Hoffman Nemiroff, "Maintenant que les clameurs se sont tues, le jeu en valait-il la chandelle?" in *Recherches Féministes*, 1995, vol. 8, no. 2, pp. 159–70.

49. Among the many works dedicated to the reorganization of racialized women's work in the 1970s and since, see Ester Boserup, *Women's Role in Economic Development*, New York: St. Martin's Press,

1970; Jules Falquet, *Pax Neoliberalia. Perspectives féministes sur la (reorganization de) la violence*. Donnemarie-Dontilly: Éditions iXe, 2016; Laurent Fraisse, Isabelle Guérin, and Madeleine Hersent, *Femmes, économie et development. De la résistance à la justice sociale*. Paris: IRD/Éditions Ères, 2011; Rhacel Salazar Parrenas, *Servants of Globalization: Women, Migration, and Domestic Work*. Stanford: Stanford University Press, 2001; Pun Ngia, *Made in China: Women Factory Workers in a Global Workforce*. Durham: Duke University Press, 2005; "Gender Alternatives in African Development: Theories, Methods, and Evidence," *Codesria*, 2005, www.codesria. org/spip/php?article362&lang=en (accessed July 2018). For a defense of a civilizing feminist point of view, see Melinda Gates, *The Moment of Lift: How Empowering Women Changes the World*. New York: Flatiron Books, 2019.

50. See NATO/EAPC (Euro-Atlantic Partnership Council) Women, Peace, and Security Policy and Action Plan 2018: www.nato.int/ nato_static_fl2014/assets/pdf/pdf_2018_09/20180920_180920-WPS-Action-Plan-2018.pdf (accessed July 2018).

In a 2017 report, NATO wrote: "on the military side, an advisor for questions of gender for the International Military Staff and an expert advisory committee (NATO Committee on Gender) responsible for promoting the integration of the gender dimension in the design, implementation, monitoring and evaluation of military policies, programs, and operations," "l'OTAN doit devenir un protecteur majeur des droits des femmes," *Geneva Tribune*, December 12, 2017.

51. International institutions have adopted policies that insist on gender equality. In the 1980s and 1990s, the World Bank and IMF widely deployed the argument that women were more responsible, to prop up their policies with regard to development and micro-credit, thereby moving attention away from their policies that had put women and men on unemployment, broken community ties, strengthened systemic violence and individualism, and placed the burden of caring for society on women. Ana Revenga and Sudhir Shetty's article "Empowering Women Is Smart Economics" is very clear on this subject, demonstrating all of the benefits the entry of women into business and work brings to the capitalist economy (in *Finance and Development*, March 2012),

www.imf.org/externa/publs/ft/fandd/2012/03/revenga.htm (accessed July 2018). In 2014, the IMF Report *Gender at Work: A Companion to the World Development Report on Jobs* described the obstacles to women's entry into the job market and the salary discrimination they face, emphasizing gender inequality. In 2018, Kristalina Georgieva, Chief Executive of the World Bank declared that "No economy can attain its full economic potential without the full and complete participation of men and women" and that the Francophone Institute for Sustainable Development, a subsidiary wing of the IFO, highlighted the essential role of women in development. www.mediaterre.org/actu,20180306233944,13.html (accessed July 2018).

52. Jules Falquet, "Genre et développement: une analyse des institutions internationales depuis la Conférence de Pékin," in Fenneke Reysoo and Christine Verschuur, *On m'appelle à régner. Mondialisation, pouvoirs et rapports de genre*. Geneva: IUE, 2003, pp. 59–90.

53. '*Pétroleuses*' were women supporters of the Paris Commune, who were accused of having burned down much of the city in 1871. The frenzied rumors that working-class women were to blame was an effect of compounded classism, sexism, and red-baiting, rather than the reporting of a true, widespread phenomena. In the 1970s, the term *pétroleuse* was reclaimed by groups of the anti-capitalist French feminist movement to signify women openly engaged in militant, revolutionary struggle. —Trans.

54. This translation of '*mal baisées*' is borrowed from Frank Wynne's translation of '*les mal baisées et les imbaisables*' in Virginie Despentes, *King Kong Theory*. London: Fitzcarraldo Editions, 2020. With thanks to Charlotte Coombe for the reference.—FV.

2.   The Evolution towards Twenty-First Century Civilizational Feminism

1. The organization, whose full name *Choisir la cause des femmes* means 'Choose the Cause of Women,' was founded by Gisèle Halimi and Simone de Beauvoir in 1971 and initially focused on the decriminalization of abortion and the criminalization of rape. Halimi remained its president until her death in July 2020. —Trans.

2. The Club des Égaux, or Club of Equals, was a think tank founded by the journalist Patrick Kessel that focused on a defense of a French secularism and "republican values." —Trans.

3. "France Plus" (1985–1997) was a movement founded by academic Arezki Dahmani, which sought to facilitate the assimilation of young people of North African descent through secularism, seeing racism as a moral flaw. —Trans.

4. La Maison de la Mutualité, the headquarters of the federation of nonprofit mutual insurers in Paris, was, until the late 1980s, a historic center for militant leftist political meetings, demonstrations, events, conferences, and other activities. In the 1970s, many feminist meetings were held there. —Trans.

5. Élisabeth Badinter, Régis Debray, Alain Finkielkraut, Élisabeth de Fontenay, and Catherine Kintzler, "Foulard islamique: Profs, ne capitulons pas!" *Le Nouvel Observateur*, November 2, 1989, reprinted by the Comité Laïcité République: www.laicite-republique.org/foulard-islamique-profs-ne-capitulons-pas-le-nouvel-observateur-2-nov-89.html (accessed July 2018). The letter begins with these words: "Only the future will tell whether the year of the Bicentennial has seen the Munich of the republican school. It is good, you say, to appease the spirits without playing into the hands of the fanatics. You would have preserved peace in both schools and society, with some concessions." (The letter's reference to Munich has become a code to refer to the 1938 settlement that permitted the German annexation of the Sudetenland and has stood since as a proof of the renouncement by democracies against rising fascism, and its goal of appeasement. In other words, accepting the veil was opening the door to similar betrayals. —Trans.)

6. Archives of the Marguerite Durand Library, consulted in March 2018.

7. Originally founded by Simone de Beauvoir as the League of Women's Rights.

8. "Lettre aux Verts", October 30, 1989, Archives of Anne Zelinski, Marguerite Durand Library, consulted in March 2018.

9. LIDF, October 8, 1989, October 15, 1989, November 6, 1989, Archives of Anne Zelinski, Marguerite Durand Library, consulted in March 2018.

10. *Journal officiel*, Debates of the National Assembly, no. 86, November 9, 1989.

11. The Marseillaise became the French National Anthem in 1879. —Trans.

12. July 14, Bastille Day in France, which commemorates the 1789 storming of Bastille prison, became a national holiday celebrating the French Revolution in July 1880. —Trans.

13. Timothée Duverger, "Le TOES 89: l'économie alternative et l'altermondialisme," August 9, 2014: www.ess.hypotheses.org/128 (accessed July 2018).

14. Archives in the Marguerite Durand Library, consulted in February 2018.

15. Debate transcripts reproduced in *Actualités Migrations*, October 30–November 12, 1989, no. 300, pp. 6–13, p. 10.

16. Ibid., p. 10.

17. Muhammad Yunus was arrested in 2011 for embezzlement.

18. See, for example, Lila Abu-Lughod, *Do Muslim Women Need Saving?* Cambridge, MA: Harvard University Press, 2013; Chandra Talpade Mohanty, *Feminism without Borders: Decolonizing Theory, Practicing Solidarity*. Durham: Duke University Press, 2003; Mwasi (Collective), *Afrofem*. Paris: Syllepse, 2018; Raquel Rosario Sanchez, "If 'White Feminism' Is a Thing, Gender Identity Ideology Epitomizes It," July 26, 2017 www.tradfem.wordpress.com/2017/08/01/if-something-like-something-%E2%80%89-gender-identity-identitical-is-really-perfectincarnation/ (accessed July 2018).

19. www.insee.fr/fr/statistics/1283207#title-block-1 (accessed July 2018).

20. Andi Zeisler, *We Were Feminists Once: From RiotGirl to CoverGirl, the Buying and Selling of a Political Movement*. New York: Public Affairs, 2016.

21. Anne Rosencher, "Alice Schwarzer: Aujourd'hui l'antiracisme prime sur l'antisexisme," *Marianne*, March 31, 2016, www.marianne.net/societe/alice-schwarzer-aujourdhui-lantiracisme-prime-sur-lantisexisme (accessed July 2018).

22. Ibid.

23. Alice Schwarzer, "The Perpetrators on NYE in Cologne were Islamists," *Breaking World News*, www.dw.com/en/alice-

schwarzer-the-perpetrators-on-nye-in-cologne-were-islamists/
a-19251564 (accessed July 2018).

24. Sarah Judith Hoffman, "Alice Schwarzer: The perpetrators on NYE in Cologne were Islamists", *DW.com*, https://www.dw.com/en/alice-schwarzer-the-perpetrators-on-nye-in-cologne-were-islamists/a-19251564 (accessed February 2021).

25. Khola Maryam Hübsch, "Thinly Veiled Racism," trans. Jennifer Taylor, January 19, 2016, www.en.qantara.de/content/cologne-new-years-eve-mob-thinly-veiled-racism (accessed July 2018).

26. Chimamanda Ngozi Adichie, *Nous sommes tous des féministes*, trans. Mona de Pracontal and Sylvie Schneiter. Paris: Gallimard, 2015. Adichie's "all", which has no gender in English, becomes masculine in French. The book was at number one for book sales on Amazon (which also offers T-shirts for men and women adorned with the slogan) for a long time.

27. Christina Sharpe, *In the Wake*. Durham: Duke University Press, 2016, p. 57.

28. BUMIDOM, *Bureau pour le développement des migrations dans le départements d'outre-mer*, was an office of the French government that, between 1963 and 1982, encouraged migration from the overseas departments of Guadeloupe, Martinique, Réunion Island, and Guiana to France. In a few years, 160,000 men and women came to France looking for work and were employed in factories, as well as in public services where French citizenship is required, but in low-paid and low-status jobs. It was the first organized migration to France, which soon targeted women to fill positions in the cleaning or care industry. They met racism and exploitation. —Trans.

29. Sara Farris, *In the Name of Women's Rights: The Rise of Femonationalism*. See also, Sara Farris, "Femonationalism and the 'Reserve' Army of Labor Called Migrant Women," *History of the Present*, 2012, vol. 2, no. 2, pp. 184–99.

30. Farris, *In the Name of Women's Rights*, p. 4.

31. See Esther M. "Reportage de la Caraïbe. Les Martiniquaises" *Histoires d'elles*, 1977 no. 5; *Cahiers du féminisme*, "Martinique, une oppression double par la domination coloniale," June–September 1979, no. 10, pp. 37–9; *Nouvelle Questions féministes*, Spring 1985: pp. 9–10, edited by Arlette Gauthier "Antillaises."

32. See, among others, Kristin Ross, *Fast Cars, Clean Bodies: Decolonization and the Reordering of French Culture*. Cambridge, MA: MIT Press, 1996; *Laver plus blanc, rouler plus vite. Modernisation de la France et décolonisation au tournant des années 60*. Paris: Flammarion, 2006; Tom Sheppard, *The Invention of Decolonization: Algerian War and the Remaking of France*. Ithaca, NY: Cornell University Press, 2008; *1962, comment l'indépendance algérienne a transformé la France*. Paris: Payot, 2012.

33. Stéphanie Condon, "Migrations antillaises en metropole," *Les cahiers du CEDREF* [online] 8–9/2000, posted online August 21, 2009, accessed September 7, 2017, www.cedref.revues. org/196 (accessed July 2018); see also the report of the Association générale des Étudiants guadeloupéens (AGEG, an activist organization), *L'émigration travailleuse guadeloupéenne en France*. Paris: L'Harmattan, 1978; Pierre Éverard, "L'intégration des infirmières antillaises dans les équipes soignantes des Hôpitaux de Paris," master's thesis, University of Lyon II, France, 1983; Fred Constant, "La politique française de l'immigration antillaise de 1946 à 1987," *Revue européenne des migrations internationales*, vol. 3, no. 3, 4th quarter, 1987.

34. Cordon, "Migrations antillaises."

35. Ibid.

36. Ibid.

37. "Family Planning: Overview of our Strategies," www. gatesfoundation.org/en/What-We-Do/Global-Development/ Family-Planning (accessed July 2018).

38. Vergès is making a reference to the 1986 polemic by French queer activist and philosopher Guy Hocquenghem: *Lettre ouverte à ceux qui sont passés du col Mao au Rotary*, which might be translated as *An Open Letter to Those Who Traded Maoism for the Rotary Club*. —Trans.

39. Journalists literally translated the name Women's Liberation Movement from the United States into the French *Mouvement de libération des femmes*.

40. This is not the place to revisit the diversity of women's groups that made up the MLF, so I am summarizing a fair amount.

41. See, for example, *Algériennes en lutte, bulletin du groupe de femmes algériennes*, December and January 1978; *Nosotras*, 1974–1976;

Pamphlet of the *Coordination des femmes noires*, 1978. During the 1980s, the Maison des femmes in Paris hosted many women's groups, including those who described themselves as racialized, queer, and lesbian. The 'Group de 6 Novembre,' a non-mixed political group, was born in November 1999 thanks to a "meeting of lesbians whose history was linked to slavery, imperialism, colonization, forced migration, all those who are generically called 'lesbians of color' in Anglo-Saxon countries." www.espace-locs. fr/2017/06 (accessed July 2018). University research on these groups has multiplied; many archives, both textual and visual, have been constituted.

42. Jesse Jackson would remark that the lead organizer of the March, Bayard Rustin, also faced prejudice in the movement, as he was gay. www.washingtonpost.com/lifestyle/women-nearly-left-off-march-on-washington-program-speaking-up-now/ 2013/08/22/54492444-0a79-11e3-8974-f97ab3b3c677_story. html?noredirect=on&utm_term=.23c485166f0f (accessed July 2018).

43. This phrase is Mary Church Terrell's. —Trans.

44. Pauli Murray, cited in Jennifer Scanlon, "Where Were the Women in the March on Washington?" *The New Republic*, March 16, 2016, www.newrepublic.com/article/131587/women-march-washington (accessed July 2018). The *New Republic* article is an extract from Scanlon's book, *Until There Is Justice*. Oxford: Oxford University Press, 2016.

45. Jeanne Theoharis, *The Rebellious Lie of Mrs. Rosa Parks*, Boston: Beacon Press, 2013.

46. See: Claudia Jones, "Femmes noires et communistes, mettre fin à une omission," *Période*, www.revueperidofe.net/author/clau-dia-jones/ (accessed July 2018). See also Carole Boyce Davies, *Left of Karl Marx: The Political Life of Black Communist Claudia Jones*. Durham: Duke University Press, 2007; Claudia Jones, *Ben Davis, Fighter for Freedom*. New York: New Century Publishers, 1954; Claudia Jones, "The Caribbean Community in Britain," *Freedomways*, vol. 4 (Summer 1964), pp. 341–57; John H. McClendon III, "Claudia Jones (1915–1964), political activist, black nationalist, feminist, journalist" in *Notable Black American Women*, Book II,

ed. Jessie Carney Smith. New York: Gale Research Inc., 1996, pp. 343–8.

47. Djamila Bouhired is a former member of the Algerian National Liberation Front (FLN) who went to trial accused of having put a bomb in a café during the War for Independence. She was arrested, raped and tortured by French paratroopers, and sentenced to die by guillotine, but ultimately her sentence was reduced to imprisonment. Her trial was made famous by a book written by Georges Arnaud and Jacques Vergès (whom she married after the war)— *Pour Djamila Bouhired* (Les Éditions de Minuit, 1957). Youssef Chahine made a film about her in 1958, *Djamila l'Algérienne*. After the war, she contributed to the journal *Révolution africaine*, participated in marches for women's rights, and was present at marches of the Hirak Movement (2019–2020). Because she has associated herself with the Palestinian cause and anti-imperialism, stubbornly refused all official and governmental positions, and always severely indicted French colonialism, she has not been included as a feminist heroine in the French feminist hegemonic narrative. —Trans.

48. Djamila Boupacha was arrested and tortured by paratroopers during the Battle of Algiers for carrying a bomb. She became a cause célèbre thank to the mobilization of Simone de Beauvoir and of her lawyer, Gisèle Halimi. Both made Boupacha into a victimized woman to be saved, (indeed, she had been brutally raped and tortured, as all Algerian women were). Their narrative did not make Boupacha an anti-imperialist or a fighter proud of her acts against the French army. None of the torturers of the thousands of Algerian women and men was brought to trial as the Évian Accords gave immunity to the French Army. —Trans.

49. On October 17, 1961, close to 30,000 Algerian women, men, and children from the outskirts of Paris demonstrated against the curfew that Maurice Papon, the chief of police had imposed. Papon authorized its police to brutally arrest and beat protesters, many died or were thrown into the Seine to drown. Fetima Bedar was the youngest of those murdered by the police. Her father, who recognized her body by her long black hair, was forced to sign a report stating she died instead by suicide. She has been remembered by anti-racist groups and her memory celebrated. —Trans.

50. Elsa Dorlin, *Se défendre, une philosophie de la violence*. Paris: La Découverte, Zones collection, 2017, loc. 270, e-book.

51. The names and actions of women active in anti-colonial feminist struggles in the French overseas departments are still barely studied and when they are, they are more than often framed as "women from overseas," in other words as belonging to a marginal chapter in the history of feminism.

52. Frantz Fanon, *Black Skin, White Masks*, trans. Charles Lam Markman. London: Pluto Press, 2008, p. 179.

53. Elaine Brown, *A Taste of Power: A Black Woman's Story*. Anchor Books, 1994. See also Robyn C. Spenser, *The Revolution Has Come: Black Power, Gender, and the Black Panther Party in Oakland*. Durham: Duke University Press, 2016.

54. Brown, *A Taste of Power*, p. 401.

55. The full text of the pamphlet, *Coordination des femmes noires 1978*, can be consulted at the Marguerite Durand Library, Reference: 099 1511.

56. Lucie Sabau, "AfroFem," feministoclic.olf.site, September 15, 2015.

57. Ibid.

58. Luc Vinogradoff, "Marche contre 'les féminicides' en Argentine et dans toute l'Amérique latine," *Le Monde*, October 19, 2016, www.lemondre.fr./big-browser/article/2016/10/19/greve-des-femmes-et-mercredi-noir-en-argentine_5016560_4832693.html (accessed July 2018).

59. The following pages are largely taken from Françoise Vergès, "Toutes les féministes ne sont pas blanches! Pour un féminisme décolonial et de marronnage," in *Philosophies des limites postcoloniales*, ed. Ahmed Boubeker and Serge Mboukou, *Le Portique*, nos. 39–40, 2017, pp. 155–77.

60. In August 2016, French Prime minister Manuel Valls opposed the naked breast of Marianne to the burkini in order to demonstrate that France was the land of women's freedom. "Valls évoque le sein nourricier de Marianne, la polémique enfle," *Ouest-France*, August 30, 2016. "Marianne"—the bust of a woman with a naked breast— was adopted as the symbol of the French Republic under the Third Republic (1871–1940). Historian Mathilde Larrère corrected the prime minister's remark by recalling that Marianne's naked breast

was a way of copying Antiquity, that its representation changed throughout the centuries, and that it has nothing to do with women's liberation. See her remarks in Assma Maad, "La leçon d'une historienne à Manuel Valls après ses propos sur Marianne et le voile," *Buzzfeed*, August 30, 2016, www.buzzfeed.com/assmamaad/une-historienne-repond-a-valls-sur-marianne-elle-a-le-sein-n?utm_term=.cgPqvrY7O#.fuwyBPWOL (accessed July 2018).

61. Louis Réard coined the term "bikini" for his two-piece bathing suit, sold in a matchbox, and marketed with the slogan: "The bikini, the first atomic bomb!" It harked back to the United States' first nuclear test on the Bikini Atoll, in the Pacific, in 1946. In total 23 nuclear bombs were tested there, forcing its inhabitants into exile. The island is uninhabitable to this day.

62. Les décodeurs, "Comment le 'burkini' est devenu la polémique du mois d'août", *Le Monde*, August 26, 2016, www.lemonde.fr/les-decodeurs/article/2016/08/26/comment-le-burkini-est-devenu-la-polemique-du-mois-d-aout_4988517_4355770.html (accessed July 2018); Jean-Claude Kaufmann, author of the book *Burkini: Autopsie d'un fait divers*, Interview, July 5, 2017, www.francetvinfo.info/societe/religion/laicite/polemique-sur-le-burkini/ (accessed July 2018); Frantz Durupt, "Le tribunal administrative de Bastia valide l'arrêté 'anti-burkini' de Sisco," *Libération*, September 6, 2016, www.liberation.fr/burkini-polemique,100641 (accessed July 2018).

63. Julien Vlassenbroek and Franceline Beretti, "Femme en bikini agressée à Reims: analyse d'un emballement sur la Toile," *rtbf info*, July 28, 2015, www.rtbf.be/info/media/detail_femme-en-bikini-agressee-a-reims-analyse-d-un-emballement-sur-la-toile?id=9042079 (accessed July 2018).

64. Ibid.

65. LCI Editorial Board, "Algérie: la révolte du bikini s'étend," LCI, August 3, 2017. The article's lead is even more suggestive: "ITSY BITSY—Since the Algerian national holiday on July 5, women have organized beach outings in the north of the country... in bikinis. One way for them to fight, in groups, against harassment and religious pressure." "Itsy Bitsy" here references the Dalida song "Itsy Bitsy Petit Bikini." (This was the French translation

of Bryan Hyland's "Itsy Bitsy Teenie Weenie Yellow Polkadot Bikini." While the lyrics are slightly different—the bikini isn't yellow in the French version—the meaning is roughly the same. —Trans.) A rough translation of the French lyrics:

> On a beach there was a pretty girl / Who was scared to get in the water / She was scared of leaving her changing room / She trembled at being seen by the neighbor / 1, 2, 3, what was she afraid of showing? / Her small, itsy bitsy, teenie-weenie, small, small, bikini.

See also Claire Tervé and Sandra Lorenzo, "Y-a-t'il eu vraiment une révolte du bikini en Algérie?" *Huffington Post*, August 7, 2017, www.huffingtonpost.fr/2017/08/07/pour-lutter-contre-lislmaisme-des-milliers-dalgeriennes-font_a_23068272 (accessed July 2018); Viviane Forson, "Algérie: les secrets d'une campagne pro-bikini," *Le Point Afrique*, July 27, 2017, www.afrique. lepoint.fr/actualites/algerie-les-secrets-dune-campagne-pro-biki-ni-27-07-2017-2146299_2365.php (accessed July 2018); H. B., "Algérie: une 'opération bikini' a t'elle été organisée sur une plage de Kabylie?" *20 Minutes*, August 8, 2017, www.20minutes. fr/monde/2114367-20170807-algerie-operation-bikini-organisee-plage-kabylie (accessed July 2018); "Nouvelle opération 'bikini' en Algérie," *BFMTV*, August 7, 2017, wwww.bfmtv.com/international/algerie-nouvelle-operation-biki-ni-pour-resist-a-la-pres-sion-religieuse-1231540.html; "Qu'est-ce que 'la révolte du bikini' en Algérie?" *BFMTV*, August 7, 2017, www.youtube.com/watch?v+Isap-PrTzHfY&feature=youtu.be (accessed July 2018).

66. Amélie James, "Algérie: qu'est-ce que la 'révolte du bikini,' mouvement citoyen et spontané," *RTL*, August 8, 2017.

67. Ibid.

68. Ibid.

69. Zohra Ziani, "Polémique sur le bikini en Algérie: des femmes veulent tourner la page," *Libération*, August 13, 2017. See also www.leparisien.fr/societe/en-algerie-ces-femmes-se-battent-pour-porter-le-biki-ni-03-08-2017-7172766.php (accessed July 2018); and Lina Kennouche, "La revolution du bikini: de la grandeur à la misère du féminisme en Algérie," *Al-Akhbar.com*, July 31, 2017, www.le-blog-sam-la-touch.overblog.com/2017/

07/la-revo-lution-du-bikini-de-la-grandeur-a-la-misere-du-feminisme-en-algerie-al-akhbar.com.html (accessed July 2018).

70. Ibid.

71. By posting these photos on her personal page and under her name, the woman gave up anonymity.

72. Céline Rousseau and Marc-Olivier Fogiel, "Strasbourg: la justice saisie contre une femme qui critique les musulmanes voilées sur Facebook," *France Blue*, August 24, 2017, www.franceblue.fr/infos/faites-divers-justice/une-complainte-deposee-strasbourg-contre-une-femme-qui-critique-sur-facebook-les-musulmanes-voiless-1503594733 (accessed August 23, 2017). The Collectif contre l'islamophobie en France (Collective Against Islamophobia in France) filed a complaint against Julia Zborovska.

73. Ibid.

74. Audre Lorde, "The Uses of Anger," *Women's Studies Quarterly*, vol. 9, no. 3, pp. 7–10, p. 7.

75. The term, *indigéniste* is the derogatory term opposed to the term *indigènes* which appeared in the 2005 *Appel des indigènes de la République* (which led to the creation of the Parti des Indigènes de la République). It does not refer to " Indigenous peoples" but to the descendants of the *indigènes* in the French colonial empire (the women and men under the status imposed by the "Code de l'indigénat"). By adopting that name, the *indigènes* of today challenge the French policy of assimilation and remind us that the French colonial politics of making non-white into *indigènes* has not ended. "*Indigénistes*" is hence used pejoratively by politicians to refer to people who denounce and analyze structural, systemic racism. —Trans.

76. Céline Pina, "L'État doit dénoncer clairement l'association Lallab, laboratoire de l'islamisme", *Le Figaro*, August 23, 2017; Pina is the founder of the Vi(r)e la République, another group created to defend French *laïcité* as a "secular, citizen, and republican movement called to fight against all totalitarianisms and for the promotion of the indispensable universality of our republican values."

77. Editorial Collective, "Stop au cyber-harcèlement contre l'association Lallab," *Libération*, August 23, 2017, www.liberation.fr/debats/2017/08/23/stop-au-cyberharcelement-islamophobe-contre-l-associa-tion-lallab_1591443 (accessed July 2018).

78. Caroline Fourest is a feminist journalist who has written ⸱ rights and is against the veil and so-called "political correct⸱ and "cancel culture."

79. See, among other studies in French addressing the specificity o⸱ Islamophobia against Muslim women, Nacira Guénif, *Des beurettes aux descendantes d'immigrants nord-africains*. Paris: Grasset, 1999; Nacira Guénif and Éric Macé, *Les Féministes et le garçon arabe*. La Tour-d'Aigues: Éditions de l'Aube, 2004; Asma Lamrabet, *Islam et Femmes, les questions qui fâchent*. Paris: Gallimard, 2018; Zahra Ali, *Féminismes islamiques*. Paris: La Fabrique, 2012. Ali's book offers "a panaroma of Islamic feminisms, in breaking with the orientalism and racism that characterize the debates about women and Islam today," responding to "the necessity of decolonizing and de-essentializing all readings of women and Islam." See also the reports of the Collectif contre l'islamophobie en France.

80. Mikelle Street, "The World's First Gender-Neutral Store Just Opened in Manhattan. Phluid Project Wants to Be a Safe Space for Clothes and Shopping," *Vice*, March 22, 2018.

81. www.thephluidproject.com/about (accessed July 2018).

82. Louise Toupin, *Le salaire du travail ménager. Chronique d'une lutte féministe internationale (1972–1977)*. Montréal: Éditions du remue ménage, 2014.

83. Christine Delphy, "Par où attaquer le 'partage inégal' du 'travail ménager'?" *Nouvelles Questions féministes*, vol. 22, no. 3, 2003, 47–71, p. 47.

84. See Louise Toupin, *Le salaire du travail ménager. Chronique d'une lutte féministe internationale (1972–1977)*. Montréal: Éditions du remue ménage, 2014; Mariarosa dalla Costa and Selma James, *The Power of Women and the Subversion of the Community*. Edinburgh: Falling Wall Press, 1975; Silvia Federici, *Caliban and the Witch: Women, the Body, and Primitive Accumulation*. New York: Autonomedia, 2004.

85. Louise Toupin, *Le salaire au travail ménager*, p. 311.

86. Silvia Federici, *Le foyer de l'insurrection. Textes pour le salaire sur le travail ménager*, ed. Le collectif féministe l'Insoumise de Genève, 1977.

87. Françoise Ega, *Lettres à une Noire. Récit antillais*. Paris: L'Harmattan, 2000, p. 137. In her book, Ega made the connection between

...ganization of the migration by the BUMIDOM
...of young women and men from post-slavery
...with the need for a racialized and gendered
...py domestic posts in French bourgeois families
...in public services.

...aZ, "The Loss of the Body: A Response to Marx's Incomplete Analysis of Estranged Labor," May 24, 2011, www.chaka85/ wordpress.com/2011/05/24/the-loss-of-the-body-a-marxist-feminist-response-to-estranged-labor (accessed July 2018).

89. The French term here—*usure*—has the double sense of wear and tear on the one hand and of usury on the other. The author plays with this dual sense in ways that have been impossible to conserve in the English. —Trans.

90. David Graeber, "Il faut réimaginer la classe ouvrière," interview by Joseph Confavreux and Jade Lindgaard, *Médiapart*, April 16, 2018.

91. Ibid.

92. Ibid.

93. Maya Mihindou, "Portrait de Fernande Bagou. Nous étions des mains invisibles." *Ballast*, 2018, www.revue-balast.fr/nous-etions-des-mains-invisibles (accessed July 2018).

94. Ibid.

95. WIEGO, "From Mozambique to Mexico, Domestic Workers are Fighting for their Rights—and Telling their Stories," June 19, 2018, www.wiego.org/blog/mozambique-mexico-domestic-workers-are-fighting-their-rights-%E2%80%94-and-telling-their-stories (accessed July 2018).

96. In 2016, even according to the cleaning company Onet (based in France, and which subcontracts cleaning jobs for hotels, railways, and hospitals, mostly employing Black women), "124 occupational disease hazards are still regrettably present, 17 more than in 2015, generating 7,092 sick days. They are linked to muscular-skeletal problems, the number one cause of occupational illness in the cleaning industry."

97. See the studies of the Centre international de recherche sur le cancer (the International Center for Cancer Research) and the Bureau européen des unions de consommateurs (The European Bureau of Consumer Unions): "The studies have shown evidence

of a link between the appearance or worsening of asthma an⟨
use of ammonia, bleach, and cleaning products, especially spray⟨
notes Nicole Le Moual, epidemiologist at Inserm, specialist i⟨
respiratory and environmental health. See also Nolwenn Weiler,
"Femmes de ménage: un métiers à hauts risques toxiques oublié
par l'écologie," *Bastamag*, March 4, 2014, www.bastamag.net/
menace-chimique-pour-les-salarie-e (accessed July 2018).

98. Jean-Michel Denis, "Dans le nettoyage, on ne fait pas du
syndicalisme comme chez Renault," *Politix*, 2009, vol. 1, no. 85,
pp. 105–26. (Île-de-France is the most populous region of France,
and it includes Paris, Versailles, and the most-visited tourist
attraction in the country, Disneyland Paris. —Trans.)

99. Synthèse de l'Observatoire de la propreté, June 2014, www.obs-
proprete.fr/pdf/E_HF_2014.pdf (accessed July 2018).

100. Le Monde de la Propreté, *Chiffres clés et actions prioritaires,
Propreté et services associés,* 2018 edition, pp. 4, 8, and 9. https://
www.monde-proprete.com/sites/default/files/0302_gie_
proprete_2018_mel_db.pdf (accessed February 2021).

101. More recently, Onet reinforced its European profile in 1999 by
joining Gegenbauer Bosse Germany and the OCS in the United
Kingdom to form Euroliance. Thanks to this operation, these
companies control 10% of cleaning services in the European
market.

102. Figures by Onet, www.fr.groupeonet.com/ (accessed July 2018).

103. "Propreté et services," www.fr.groupeonet.com/Nos-metiers/
proprete-et-services (accessed July 2018).

104. Onet, "Life is Beautiful," January 20, 2016, www.youtube.com/
watch?v=pSbLU-Vvn2lu (accessed July 2018).

105. "Madame Gueffar, ancienne salariée d'Onet," testimony,
Fakirpresses, March 29, 2016, www.youtube.com/watch?v=W4k
DdM1xvmA (accessed July 2018).

106. www.krishnapriyade-sign.com/ (accessed July 2018).

107. Arturo Escobar, *Sentir-Penser avec la Terre. L'écologiue au-delà de
l'Occident*, trans. L'Atelier La Minga (collective). Paris: Éditions
du Seuil, 2018, p. 180.

108. Extract from "Manifeste de L'Atelier IV," Performance curated by
Françoise Vergès, Paris, June 12, 2017.

Index